PREPARING FOR REUNION

Adopted people, adoptive parents and birth parents tell their stories

First published in 1994 by
The Children's Society
Edward Rudolf House
Margery Street
London WC1X 0JL

A catalogue record for this book is available from the British Library.

ISBN 0 907324 78 9

Typeset and printed by
The Grange Press
Butts Road, Southwick, Sussex

PREPARING FOR REUNION

Adopted people, adoptive parents and birth parents tell their stories

Editorial team:

Julia Feast, Post Adoption and Care: Counselling and
  Research Project
Michael Marwood, Norwich Project
Sue Seabrook, East Midlands Children's Resource
  Team
Annabel Warbur, Publications Editor
Liz Webb, Adoption Project Tunbridge Wells

Illustrations by Guy Parker-Rees

The Children's Society
MAKING LIVES WORTH LIVING
A VOLUNTARY SOCIETY OF THE CHURCH OF ENGLAND
AND THE CHURCH IN WALES
Charity Registration No. 221124.

CONTENTS

INTRODUCTION

This book is written by some of the experts in the field of adoption: those people who have been adopted, have had a child adopted or have adopted a child themselves. It is primarily intended for people who are personally involved in the adoption circle, but we hope it will be of value and interest to other people too and also to professionals working in this field. The purpose of this collection of experiences is to share with others in the same situation the elations, anxieties, joys and dilemmas involved in searching for and meeting birth relatives. For most of the contributors, their search and reunion are relatively recent events. Their accounts therefore reflect their own ways of preparing for reunion and the immediate outcomes rather than the long-term effect of their renewed relationships.

We hope that whether you are an adopted person and are embarking on your own search, an adoptive parent, a birth relative, or anyone else concerned with any part of the searching process, you will be able to identify with some of what is written. We believe that the accounts speak for themselves and we have only edited them to protect identity and avoid repetition. You may or may not agree with what the contributors have written, you may do things differently, but this is their story.

During the 1960s and 70s, The Children's Society was one of the largest adoption agencies operating in England and Wales and made more that 11,000 adoption placements. The Children's Society of the 1990s is very different, and although it is still an adoption agency, the number of children it places each year is very small. All of these are either children with special needs or older children.

Nevertheless, many of those thousands of children placed by the Society in the 1960s and 70s are now approaching the Society for help in tracing their birth families. Those of us who specialize in this area of work have between us supported many hundreds of people in their search for information about their past and possibly a subsequent reunion with their birth family. We also work closely with adoptive parents and birth relatives. It is from this work and experience that *Preparing for Reunion* grew. In addition to the voices of those who have experienced the process of tracing and reunions at first hand, we have added our perspective as professional birth records counsellors.

Adoption was legalized in England and Wales in 1926. For years it was seen as a solution to two problems. First, it offered the chance of having a child to married couples who were unable to conceive a child of their own. Second, it provided a safe and secure family to children of women – usually unmarried – who were deemed unable to raise their babies themselves because they lacked a husband, financial support, a house, or their family's and society's approval to do so.

Only healthy babies could be adopted, so adoption agencies collected just enough information about the birth family to confirm this. Much secrecy surrounded baby placements. This was thought to be in everyone's best interests, and all the parties were assured that this secrecy would be permanently maintained. This did not, however, stop adopted people from asking about themselves and their origins.

Some adopted people have described themselves as feeling like a jigsaw puzzle with a piece missing. As their demands for information grew louder, so society's attitudes to adoption and the need for secrecy when children were born to unmarried women were also changing. Adopted people's need for access to information about themselves and their right to a complete sense of identity were eventually acknowledged and were reflected in subsequent legal changes.

Under the provisions of the Children Act 1975, adopted people were allowed, from the age of 18, to obtain a copy of their original birth certificate and thus the name(s) of their birth parent(s) and their place of birth.[1]

Staff of adoption agencies had to tackle questions such as whether they should reveal information given under a promise of confidentiality, for example, the identity of a birth father who was said not to know he had fathered a child.

Most of the people whose accounts are included in this book

---

[1] In Scotland, young people were given this right from the age of 17 under the provisions of the Adoption Act (Scotland) 1978. In Northern Ireland, the Adoption (Northern Ireland) Order 1987, implemented in 1989, allowed access to original birth certificates for those aged 18 or over.

were involved in baby adoptions made before 1975. When the placement was made, therefore, there was no possibility of there being any further contact between the adopted person and their birth family. Many of the accounts talk about the profound impact that the change in the law has had, as it has given them access to information they previously thought would be withheld for ever.

If you have been adopted, you may have been thinking about obtaining information and considering a possible reunion for many years. This is not a step-by-step guide to finding your family of origin but an attempt at emotional preparation by raising and thinking about the issues involved. Not all adopted people choose to seek information about their family.

For some adopted people, it is enough simply to know who they are by name, the name of their birth mother and where they came into the world. For others, including some who thought originally that they only wanted basic information, this produces a need to know more about why they were given up for adoption and to find and meet members of their family of origin.

If you seek counselling about your birth records, you will probably have thought about the possible outcome. Some people discover that they have been brought up in a family very different from their original one and are faced with huge adjustments. This may be particularly true for black children placed with white families and for children placed in families with a different religion. In the 1960s and 70s little consideration was given to the importance of matching race, culture and religion. A recent example of this was a man who was adopted into a Christian family who later discovered he was of Jewish birth.

Some people discover incredible coincidences, like the man who took his family on holiday to the same hotel in a coastal resort every year for 14 years and when he went for counselling found he had been born in a nursing home around the corner from this hotel. Some people discover clandestine family relationships, like the woman adopted by her birth mother's sister.

Some adopted people feel that they need to keep their intentions and search secret from their adoptive parents. Others have the full support of their adoptive parents and are even accompanied by them on their journey. Many feel that having a friend, relative or a counsellor they can turn to helps them get through the difficulties and confusion of merging the past with the present and the future.

Many of those who come forward for counselling about their birth records have thought of the effect their search may have on their birth mother and have realized that if she is now married and has other children, her family may or may not know of their existence.

Re-establishing contact with a birth family can be a positive and fulfilling experience but it may also bring its own dilemmas. How many adopted people realize, for example, how their search might affect their partner or children? The search, the outcome, the relationship with a birth parent may become so all-consuming and fiercely personal as to exclude, perhaps only temporarily, the closest members of the adopted person's family. What of the birth parent or sibling who becomes emotionally over-dependent on their newly found child or brother/sister? What sort of relationship will develop? Will it be friendship? Will it be love?

From the point of view of birth relatives, reunions raise many different issues and may bring with them a raking-up of painful past memories and secrets. Many birth relatives talk of an overwhelming grief and sense of loss that they have kept hidden for years, unable to speak about it to anyone.

As an adoptive parent, you may wish to support your child but you may also fear losing him or her and worry about what may happen. Experience tells us that the bond and commitment forged during the childhood years is usually strong enough to accommodate another relationship in the life of the adoptive family, although often time is needed for readjustment. Nevertheless, as an adoptive parent, you may not have been prepared for the changes the Children Act 1975 has brought about and you may not agree with them.

In the first section of this book, we have tried to address the questions most commonly asked of birth records counsellors and to include relevant quotes from people with first-hand experience of the tracing process. The second section is devoted to longer accounts from adopted people, adoptive parents and birth parents of their experiences of searching and reunions. The final section contains extracts from a diary kept by Lucy, who searched for her birth family when she was 18. Her diary charts both the sequence of events and her changing emotions over a ten-month period. Lucy's adoptive mother's account is also included.

The book can be read as a whole, or you may prefer to begin with specific sections written by or addressed to adopted people, adoptive parents or birth parents. Yet each part of it is relevant to all those in the adoption circle, as part of the emotional preparation for reunion is an understanding of how other people will be affected. Each reunion and its outcome is, of course, intensely personal and it is impossible to prepare yourself fully. We hope, however, that you will find an echo and a response to some of your own particular questions and concerns. In reading what others have written of their own experiences of searches and reunions, you may feel better prepared for your own.

FIRST THOUGHTS

This section addresses some of the questions most commonly asked by adopted people, adoptive parents and birth parents. It is not possible to provide simple answers. We hope, however, that our own experience as birth records counsellors and the reflections of some of those we have worked with, will help you to consider the issues raised by the tracing process.

PUTTING THE PIECES TOGETHER

Adopted people

Developing a clear sense of self-identity is an integral part of
growing up. For most people, it is a complex process. For people who are adopted, it can often be an even more difficult
task and one that may become increasingly preoccupying during their teenage years.

Inherited physical features are very much part of being a
family. Colour of hair and eyes, shape of nose, height, build
and mannerisms may identify a child with one or other of his
or her parents. So, too, may elements of their temperament or
their interests.

Despite awareness of the need to consider physical and cultural features when placing children for adoption, it is not an
aspect that was always consciously given a high priority in the
past (especially when placing older children). People who have
been adopted may grow increasingly aware of being 'different'
from their adoptive family. This may be heightened even more

when children have been placed in cultures different from their original ones.

· As an adopted person, you may have very little information about your birth family. In our experience of birth record counselling, a search for completeness and a missing past is the most common factor in adopted people's decisions to find out more about their birth family.

"I feel an incomplete person, a part of me is missing ... I don't know who my mother is. Who do I look like? ...my mother or my father? Do we share the same likes and dislikes? Do I have any brothers and sisters that I don't know about? There are so many unanswered questions."

"I think that it was because the information was so sketchy that my birth parents were always on my mind. Questions kept going round and round in my head: what are they like? who are they? I knew that unless I found out who they were or at least got some information, I would never be comfortable."

"I had always wanted to find my mother just to let her know that I was alright and happy. I never thought I would carry on seeing her. I wanted to meet my father more out of curiosity, to see what he looked like.

I have now met both of them. Having met my father, I feel that I have some sort of peace about my identity, some sense of my Caribbean half."

For some people, there can be a sense of unreality concerning information they do already have about their origins until they see for themselves some tangible evidence, such as their birth certificate.

"My 30th birthday was approaching and as my adoptive mother had died in 1975, and my adoptive father in 1982, I felt that the time was right for me to find out the truth about my origins. Just basic questions that any 'natural' child could have answered by its mother. Why did I have blue eyes, brown hair, why was I born with a rash on my face, was I breast or bottle-fed? Just very basic information that I wanted so that I could build up an early medical history and more importantly an identity.

As I had cleared my parents' house out in 1982, I had found a letter from The Children's Society regarding the processing of my adoption and had found my name entered on this document as Terry Blackley. I had had this document in my posses-

9

sion for five years but had not followed it up. As anyone can apply for a copy of an entry of birth, I duly sent off for a copy birth certificate of this person who at this time was totally alien to me and with whom I did not identify. I knew the certificate would reveal the name of the mother and possibly the father of this Terry Blackley, the address of the parents at the time of birth, the place of birth, and the date and place of registration. I should stress at this point that this was an unusual way for an adopted child to obtain a copy of his natural birth certificate and in hindsight I would not recommend it.

Anyway, six weeks later the envelope popped through the letterbox. I did not open it for about 48 hours, as I was not prepared emotionally for the information contained on the certificate, but at the same time was eager to know. When the time came, I gingerly removed it from the envelope and opened it up. The information revealed therein gave me a feeling of absolute awe. For the first time I was able to identify with this unknown person named Terry. I was able to see on an official form that I actually did exist and was just like everybody else."

In the majority of cases, adopted people start with a search for their mother. People are also often excited at the prospect of finding half- or step-brothers or sisters. Having found their mother, however, the curiosity and sometimes the focus of the searching may move across to their father. Sadly, there is usually far less information about the father, who may not even be aware that he has a child. It is our experience at The Children's Society, however, that where putative fathers do know about the child, once they are traced and approached their responses are usually positive.

Birth relatives
Until recently, it has been the norm that adopted people are the ones who trace and the birth relatives wait either expectantly or in trepidation, usually a lot of both. Like adopted people, many birth relatives also have a need to 'put the pieces together', to know whether their child is alive and well, and to let them know that they have not been forgotten. For some, this may be a way of coming to terms with their grief in having given their child up for adoption.

"Can a woman forget her own baby and not love the child she bore? Maybe for a time, but so many things trigger off the

grief of parting and loss. Sometimes I just sob when a re-minder comes up in my memory. I press down feelings and grief because that is what I have learnt to do."

Some birth mothers need to feel reassured that they did the right thing and want to make certain that their child knows why they were adopted.

"Simon was always in my thought and prayers. Now we have a chance to get together and I can put him in the picture over things that happened."

WHEN SHOULD I SEARCH?

Many people start searching because they want to find more information about themselves. Some people may also hope to develop a friendship with their birth family. You will need to consider carefully whether this is the right time for you to begin your own search.

There are a number of situations or events that commonly trigger adopted people to search. These include reaching their 18th birthday, a need for medical history particularly if they are about to parent a child, seeing a programme on television, meeting another person who has traced, wanting to reassure their birth parent that they are well and happy, and feeling settled enough in themselves to cope with whatever the search may reveal.

Birth parents will usually wait until their offspring are over 18, but they might try to find some peace of mind by getting news of their child at an earlier stage through the adoption agency that made the placement. If you are a birth parent, it is possible for you to place letters at any time on your child's file, which is held by the agency that made the placement.

The following adopted people describe what prompted them to begin their search for their birth families.

"It is only now, when I feel I've got to the age when I've got all my teenage problems away and I'm fairly secure in myself, that I feel I need to trace my birth mother. I don't regret starting to trace. It is something I thought about over a long period. I feel quite comfortable about it but I have not made contact yet.

I think you've got to decide in your own mind before you make contact what you are hoping to get out of it. It is no good going in there because you've got problems at home and expect it is going to be wonderful to have a new family. If you've got problems with one family you have probably got twice as many with two families."

"I have always known that I was adopted, but always held resentment for my birth parents. I think it was the feeling of not being wanted, rejected, and thinking in a very selfish way that my birth parents could not have really cared about me that much. It was only when I was about 22 that my attitude changed. I had gone through all the changes of life. My adoptive father and only grandparent had died when I was a teenager and my adoptive sister had left home."

"..when I became pregnant with my first daughter my attitude changed, partly due to all the medical questions I was asked to which I did not have the answers. However, I did nothing further until after my second child was born."

"I have always wanted to find out more about my birth parents. When I was 16 I felt I really wanted to look for my Mum, maybe because I was about the same age as she was when she had me. I was living away from my adoptive parents in a children's home and there was an officer in charge there in whom I confided a lot. She was very good and helped me a lot. People took me seriously and understood what I was going through. They never turned round and said to me 'you are being pathetic', but they explained why I was too young to trace.

But as the year has gone on (I'll be 18 soon) and as I am coming up to the time when I can find out more about her, I'm thinking that perhaps I ought to wait. I don't want to rush into anything and find out things I don't want to. I'd rather get it right. But I'm not in any hurry to do so."

"...At the age of 26 I felt I could cope with any rejection that could be involved in my tracing my parents... ...My second meeting with my counsellor took place a couple of weeks later. She had warned me to be prepared, but no one can prepare you for the truth ..."

WHAT AM I
LETTING MYSELF IN FOR?

Adopted people
It is important that the risks inherent in contacting relatives
separated by adoption are fully acknowledged before opening
a possible Pandora's box. Even if it is a successful reunion, it
is also a time of emotional stress and adjustment as the past
and present come face to face. In our experience of birth
records counselling, it is advisable for people to feel reasonably secure in themselves when making contact, as the
process can raise as many issues as it solves.

However much you try to prepare yourself, it is difficult to
predict the feelings and emotions that tracing and reunions
will evoke. But you do have to consider how you might cope
with the multiplicity of relationships that a reunion may
bring, what impact the reunion may have on your existing
relationships, and also how you might feel if you don't like
your new family. These are important considerations for all
the parties involved in an adoption.

Adopted people, birth families and adoptive families will all
have their own set of fears and anxieties. For adopted people,
perhaps the worst fear is that of rejection. Many fear that
their birth parent will not want any contact with them. Many

15

others worry that even if their birth parent agrees initially to have contact, he or she might reject them after their reunion.

Jane was 35 years old when she contacted the Society for her birth records. She wanted to receive background information, but also to find her birth parents. Jane had a very happy adoption and was in regular contact with her adoptive family. Her adoptive parents supported her need to find out more about her origins and gave her all the information they had about her birth family.

Jane was pleased to receive so much information from her records; it helped to fill the gaps. However, she learned that her birth mother had already contacted the Society to leave her current address in case Jane ever made contact.

Jane was delighted, but at the same time felt reticent. She hadn't expected her search to end so quickly, but also felt she needed more time to consider the implications for contact. She believed that her reunion would be more complex than most. Jane was gay and had been living with her partner for five years. Although her adoptive family had accepted that Jane was gay, she was aware that some people had not.

She wanted to meet her birth mother and siblings, and wanted to be open about her relationship with Sue. She was in a dilemma – when should she tell her birth family?

Eventually she decided that she would not be able to cope with being rejected, so she withdrew from the search.

Many people will, however, feel that the risk of rejection is worth taking in order to have a chance of finding out more about themselves and their background. The mere fact of having up to date information, whether good or bad, can often have a releasing effect.

Birth parents

As a birth parent, you too may fear rejection. If now married with a family of your own, you may also be concerned about any changes within your family, particularly if the adoption has been kept secret. Will your eldest child feel 'less special', for example, if they find they are no longer 'the eldest'?

Cynthia's account shows the conflicting emotions that first contact from a child given up for adoption may bring:

"My own wishes were quite simple. Of course I wanted contact with him again. I wanted reassurance that he was coping

with life, that my decision to have him adopted hadn't blighted him in any way. I was also very curious to know what he was like. I also felt that it wasn't 'fair' not to write to him. I thought that it would be like another rejection, if he felt that his adoption had already been one rejection. I didn't understand why he wanted to have any contact with me, and I didn't want to hurt him, so I agreed to write to him, giving details about my family and background. I didn't tell him that I had later married his father and that our daughter was his sister. I thought at first that he might only want details about his background."

Adoptive parents
If you adopted your child before 1975, you may be finding it hard to come to terms with the changes in the law. Unlike parents who adopted children after 1975, you were not prepared when the adoption first took place for the possibility of your child tracing their birth family, or being traced by a birth relative.

For many adoptive parents, the process of tracing can be a stressful time. You may fear that if your child traces it will alter their relationship with you. You may feel excluded from the process of the forming of a new relationship. You may be worried that your child will get hurt in the process of tracing. These are by no means unnatural or unusual feelings.

Some of the anxieties felt by many adoptive parents are voiced here by Sandra as she looks back at her daughter's reunion with her birth family.

"Although I am successfully coming to terms with the idea that we are not Laura's only family, I feel some disquiet that the adoptive family ceases to have any 'rights' once the child is 18. This is no doubt inevitable, since he/she is an adult and can dictate the terms and the pace. As Laura reminded me, she could have gone behind our backs, which while it would have been out of character, clearly insinuated 'it's none of your business'! However, I feel strongly that the adoptive family should have the right to expect some loyalty from the child. Perhaps like Laura they underestimate the depth of love and commitment which the adoptive parents give, in the belief that they are 'different' from other children. Having undervalued themselves, they do not expect the adoptive family to mind 'losing' them. Certainly Laura thought we were impervious to hurt.

I understand that adopted children need to find their birth parents in order to feel 'completeness'. But I am sure that I am not the only adoptive mother who finds it difficult to overcome the sense of failure which results from her child's need to seek an alternative."

Another adoptive parent writes:
"Suddenly I felt drained and empty. For weeks I had been going along with Kate, excited for her, and suddenly it was over and I felt very alone. I would have liked to put the brakes on then and not let it go any further but that would have been selfish, as after all, we had shown the birth family a lovely daughter and granddaughter. I have always discussed every-thing with my children and explained to Kate how I felt. I said that part of me was scared of losing her. She hastily assured me that that would never happen. She thanked me for making it all possible and said that she now felt 'complete'.

Since then she has visited her birth family once with her boyfriend and has met her aunt. However much environment plays a part in our upbringing, the hereditary factor is very strong and they have a lot in common. I feel close to Kate's new family and hope that we will continue to keep in touch. After all, we are all part of Kate's life."

It is good if adoptive parents are able to consider the implications of tracing and reunions and to prepare themselves in advance for the fact that, if the reunion is successful, they may have to 'share' their child, which may not feel comfortable at first. It may be helpful for all parents to remind themselves that no one 'owns' their children and that one of the roles of parents is to help their children grow towards independence.

In our experience, an adopted person is likely to have divided loyalties. The process of tracing is usually made much easier for them if they know that their adoptive parents sup-port them and understand that their need to find out about their origins is natural and is no reflection on their parenting.

"I am very close to my adoptive mother and I'm extremely grateful that she was so helpful and willing about me finding my birth mother. Until the time we first met my birth mother, she knew that I was her daughter and nobody else's. After a little reminding and reassuring she could feel this again."

The key towards making maximum success out of reunions

is to build up new relationships slowly. Don't rush into something that is going to make you feel uncomfortable. Consider the implications with a counsellor or friend, who can help you to take one step at a time.

The following was written by an adopted person after he had traced his birth mother, who refused to have any contact with him. He later had a successful reunion with his father.

"To the adoptee, do what is in your heart
To the birth mother, don't be afraid
To the adoptive parent, brothers and sisters, support them,
don't misunderstand or be disappointed, it's simply the natural
instinct of needing to know."

AM I BEING DISLOYAL?

Many adopted people feel that tracing their birth parents is being disloyal to their adopters. Many therefore put off tracing their birth relatives until their adoptive parents have died, by which time there is an increased risk that some of their birth relatives may also have died. Alternatively, they may trace secretly, being afraid of hurting their adoptive parents or implying that they have not been good enough.

Some adopted people who go ahead and trace their birth family have to cope with feeling torn between their two families. The attitude of adopters and what they communicate to the adopted person about tracing will therefore be crucial to how, if and when an adopted person searches for people from the past. Many adoptive parents quite naturally fear losing their unique relationship with their child. Yet, when the adoptive parent can give 'permission' for their son/daughter to find out more about his/her birth parents, this gives tremendous support to the adopted person, and may in fact preserve and strengthen the relationship between them.

"Throughout the tears and rows we have SURVIVED and family relationships have now returned to their former easy, happy state. The bond is now even stronger. I feel so lucky, so fortunate, so blessed that it should be so. It proves to me just what the 'family' is all about and that there is nothing in the world as valuable as love.

Amanda is now a 'complete person'. She is able to go forth and cope in a mature and stable way with her own life, career and future, and above all is just so HAPPY. I find it difficult to believe that in the depths of her searching we all felt so insecure, but now I am so very proud of each member of my family. We are here, we did make it and we are as one."

This point is emphasized by Stefan and Lucy.

Stefan writes: *"I still see my birth mother on a regular basis, and I am happy in that I have benefited from this experience, but I know that deep down I will never be able to build a bond like the one between the parents who actually brought me up through the good times and the bad."*

Lucy waited until her adoptive parents had died before tracing, and writes: *"I wish in my heart that my adoptive parents could be here now so I could give them a hug and tell them I love them so much and that my searching out my birth mother has made no difference to the way I feel for them."*

SHOULD I KEEP THIS A SECRET?

It is a common feeling for those involved in adoption to wish to keep their search a secret. Indeed, secrecy was often at the root of an adoption: in the past, unmarried pregnant women were often hidden away, sent on 'holiday' to have their baby. The baby may have been born and adopted in secret. Sometimes even the grandparents did not know about the pregnancy. It is not unknown for a second child born to the mother to be given the name of the child who was adopted. If not kept a secret from a future husband, a child of the past is often a secret from other children in the family.

For adopters, too, there may be secrets. Some may have tried to pretend that their adopted children are their own flesh and blood and may have concealed the truth for many years.

Adopted people often find it difficult to tell their own natural children that they are adopted. Many have traced in secret and do not want to tell their adoptive parents for fear of seeming to be disloyal. So the burden of secrets grows. It is important to consider the implications of keeping secrets and the effect this will have on others when the truth gets out.

The following accounts highlight some of the difficulties and burdens secrecy may cause.

"I haven't told my adoptive mother about my approach to The Children's Society. (My adoptive father died when I was 14.)

I would like to tell her very much, mainly because I feel so guilty about it, but as yet I have not found the courage to do so. At first, I didn't say anything to her as there wasn't much to tell but as with all secrets, the longer it has gone on, the harder it is to tell. Whilst I knew at a fairly young age that I was adopted, it was always to be kept 'a secret', so much so that only a handful of people know that I am adopted. And so for some reason, the whole subject of adoption is very emotional, and even the most basic of discussions on this subject with my adoptive mother is very difficult."

"My mother had three daughters after my adoption – the eldest only 14 months younger than me. They had not been told of my existence, and my mother decided to tell the girls after I had made contact. Talk about drama! Tears, shock and dramatics were the order of the day. I rang my mother on the day she told them, and she put her middle daughter Alison on the phone. I have never felt so inadequate in my life."

Roger's account illustrates the way in which secrecy can become more and more complicated with time, and a greater burden to carry:

"It never entered my head that I would tell my adoptive parents about my search – I didn't want to cause an upset, particularly as I didn't know at first whether anything would come of it. Originally I never thought there would be any possibility of contact, but when I traced my family I found they lived within 20 miles of my adoptive parents. I am still unable to tell them that I have found my birth relatives. I'm afraid that it will spoil our relationship. Because so much time has passed now since I first started tracing, it is a subject that is now even more difficult to bring up. It is easier to let things be.

When I started tracing I had no children, but now I have a daughter. It is becoming more complicated to keep secrets. It was alright when my daughter was small, although she does not as yet know her father is an adopted person. I'd prefer to leave it that way, although I do realize that some time in the future there is going to come a crunch time. I'm afraid that as my daughter gets older she might relay information to my adoptive parents. I want to protect them from being hurt. I am their son and my daughter is their granddaughter.

As an additional complication to this secrecy, when I first appeared in my birth family, my sister was put in a predicament. She was brought up by her maternal grandparents and her mother was treated as her sister. So the people my sister's children believed to be their grandparents were in fact their great-grandparents."

WHAT IF THEY DON'T WANT TO KNOW?

One of the reasons that some people do not search or make contact with their birth parents is the fear of being rejected. It is impossible to predict who this is going to happen to, but it is something that you should consider. Rejections can occur for many reasons. Birth mothers may be afraid to tell their husbands and children; they may feel that they made a decision years ago and do not want to go back.

Rejection does not just apply to the adopted person. It may come from any party; for example a birth mother rejected by her adopted child, or rejection by brothers and sisters.

It is not uncommon for people's initial response to be a refusal to have any contact, perhaps because of shock and fear of what it may lead to. Inevitably, this often feels like a personal rejection. It is important to remember, however, that it is not you they are rejecting but rather the situation and the memory that it arouses of past and painful events.

Given support and time to think it over, some people change their minds and agree to establish some sort of contact. Often, adopted people are not initially looking for a meeting with their birth relatives but simply a chance to let them know that they are alive and well and perhaps to exchange letters. This may or may not develop into further and more direct contact.

Angie is of mixed parentage and was brought up in a white adoptive family. Her birth mother was white and from an upper middle class family. She describes here her feelings when her birth mother refused to have any contact with her. She later went on to have a successful reunion with her birth father.

"I'm a very realistic person – without being negative – and had considered every possibility: my birth mother may be dead (with this thought comes a sense of sorrow but also relief – no danger of repeated rejection!); she may not want to know at all; she may be ashamed – of herself and/or me; I may be her darkest secret (with this thought comes a sense of responsibility – will I cause ructions in her happy family?). And then there's confusion and guilt: do I care if I upset her life and create havoc in the hearts of her husband or my half-brothers and -sisters?

I hoped, of course, that she might understand my need, my desire and curiosity, but I also understood that whatever her thoughts and feelings the dominant feeling would be fear or even horror: the past that came back to haunt her! I suspected that she wouldn't want to meet me, but hoped that she would allow me to communicate directly with her and eventually maybe even correspond with me.

By this time I had built up a close and solid trust and friendship with my adoption counsellor. We talked at length about how to go about it and the possible response. I remember saying to her that you can be as intellectually prepared as you like, but preparing emotionally for either a positive or negative response is nearly impossible. I was as prepared as I could be. I may even have been more frightened of a positive response than a negative one!

You may have guessed by now that the response was negative. Not just a bit negative, VERY negative! The sentence that sticks in my head, heart and throat is: "as far as I am concerned, she's not my daughter". I marvel at a mother being able to think this of a child that she bore, much less express it. I put it down to her fear. Fundamentally, I believe that that's what it is, but I think that the reasons for it are obviously manifold.

Initially I felt deep disappointment, bitter resentment and blind fury! I was angry for days, weeks, months. I'm still angry 16 months later. I think I understand why her response was so final and negative, but I resent her cowardice – although I try not to judge her.

I believe for her the major fear is that I'm black (or 'mixed-race' as I suppose I'm officially called – though the white person's world in which I live sees me as a black woman by virtue of the fact that I'm not white).

... I believe that it's a hard task for adoption counsellors to prepare adoptees for rejection. To me, the most important thing was to consider every possibility, be angry or elated in advance. To really think how I may feel in the situation and also to try to imagine how it might be to be in her shoes. To recognize that rejection is more a reflection of her, than a judgement of me.

Obviously, a sense of self-worth and recognition of one's individuality is essential for happiness in everyone, regardless of whether they're adopted or not. It's hard for all of us, but we have to recognize as adoptees that our strength lies in our identity within, not in whether we are acknowledged by a parent or not. I feel that this too is something that counsellors can remind us about before the ordeal of acceptance or rejection."

Terry describes how he felt when his birth mother refused to have any contact with him:

"Whilst I was prepared for the worst, I hoped for the best. A date I will never forget is 1 November 1989. This was the day a letter popped through my door. It was a letter from a firm of London solicitors. The letter read as follows:

"We have been instructed by your mother who has learned of your efforts to contact her. We have been asked to inform you that she has no wish for you to contact her and wishes no contact with you, however hard you may find this to accept. We have been asked to make it clear that your mother is alive and well and happily married. We are instructed that the disclosure of your birth would cause not only distress to her, but other members of her family were this to be revealed now or in the future. Yours faithfully"

I was totally devastated, to say the least. I would have been able to accept it more easily if she or my grandfather could have taken the trouble to write a brief letter to me explaining the reasons why, although they were and still are blatantly obvious. I understood what she would have gone through both physically and emotionally. I have since learned, quite recently from an elderly adoptive aunt, that at my adoption hearing my birth mother and her own mother were both in Court. My birth mother was in tears. I too have cried and understand the pain, I too felt it for so many years and still do.

The ensuing month saw me for at least 75 per cent of the time permanently drunk. Hopes and aspirations of adopted people finding parents as are portrayed on programmes such as Surprise, Surprise *and various documentaries over the years only show the good reunions and not the disappointments. I did write back to my mother asking why, this time directly to her home address. The reply came back via a private detective that my mother did not care for me, never had and never would, and that her husband was particularly angry. In the meantime, I had been in touch with Robert Kilroy-Silk to have the false pictures of TV put right in people's minds, for them to know what can be in store for them. Counselling services do not prepare people harshly enough for what can be the greatest disappointment in their lives."*

Like Angie, Terry did later go on to have a successful reunion with his father.

WILL MY RECORDS STILL BE AVAILABLE?

Adoption records are required by law to be kept for 75 years. You should, however, be aware that in rare cases records have been lost through fire, flood and accident over the years. These losses, which can be extremely distressing and frustrating, have occurred both in adoption agencies and court premises. Nobody should underestimate the effect of the loss of records, as they are often the only way forward in the search.

"When I contacted the agency for my records, I never expected to be told that they'd been destroyed by fire. I can't describe how desperate I feel because I don't know where to go from here to find out who I am."

Shirley found out when she was 20 that she was adopted. She had made attempts to trace her birth family on and off since 1975. She found out that the County Court papers were burned during a blitz in London. She did not know which agency she was adopted through. After writing to several possible adoption agencies, The Children's Society located the agency that had her records, only to discover that her file had been destroyed by fire.

The following extract from a letter from a birth mother describes the frustration she felt at being being unable to obtain records of her daughter.

"I would appreciate your help. I am a birth mother ... In my attempts to trace my daughter's records and sealed file I have contacted many, many people but none have been able to offer me any help. I wish to leave a note on my daughter's sealed file, giving my name and address in case she attempts to trace me. To do so I must first discover where her sealed file is being held and by whom, and I have drawn a total blank.

I was resident in a Mother and Baby Home. I have discovered it was closed down in 1977 and those responsible for the records have no idea where they are, no one has seen them since. The Society made every attempt to help me, providing possible contact phone numbers.

I phoned them all and drew blanks. To date I've found it impossible to find my daughter's records and sealed file. Worse, the department responsible for their safe keeping can offer no help."

WHAT WILL BE IN MY RECORDS?

When the Children Act 1975 was introduced, adopted people were given the right to know their original name, their birth mother's name and the name of the agency that placed them (if this was known). Any other information on adoption records is given at the discretion of the adoption agency concerned. At The Children's Society, we try to share as much information as possible.

The content of adoption records varies greatly and there may not be much more detail in them than has been given to your adopters at the time of your adoption. The longer ago the adoption, generally the more sparse the information. The records should, however, contain an address of where your birth mother was living at the time of your adoption and often names, ages and addresses of other relatives.

Records were written by social workers without any expectation of anyone outside the agency reading them and they reflect the social values and the prejudices of the individual and of the time. Subjective comments about the birth circum-stances made by social workers who compiled the records can sometimes be quite hurtful. This applies particularly to earlier records when illegitimacy tended to be seen as a social disgrace. Records may also contain remarks that are racist.

Ideas about whether or not a child was suitable for adoption were also very different and babies may have been deemed 'unadoptable' for reasons that nowadays seem very minor.

One of the most precious items that is sometimes found in the records is a handwritten letter from the birth mother, either at the time of the adoption or later. It might explain why she felt it was best for her child to be adopted. Sometimes the letter includes a current address and expresses a wish for contact with the adopted person. Unfortunately sometimes the original letter has been destroyed after records have been transferred onto microfilm.

"I found out my name, my parents' names and the rest of my family's details. I also found out I had a brother and sister! A lot to take in at one go, I can tell you.

After the meeting, I asked if any contact had been made from my mother. A very long pause occurred and I was told she had been in contact and she wanted to meet me. "Wow!" I guess was the first word I said! I couldn't believe it had all happened so quickly."

In cases such as this one, it is important that people still stand back and think about the issues before they embark on a relationship they are not ready for.

You should find enough details on your records to enable you to go forward in your search and to obtain a copy of your own and your mother's birth certificates, if you have not already done so through the General Register at St Catherine's House, London. There are usually descriptions giving details of your mother's physical appearance and her inter-ests. Information about the medical history of your birth fam-ily is varied and usually only highlights significant conditions.

Although it is hoped that the records reflect the true situa-tion at the time of the adoption, there are occasions when birth relatives have given incorrect information in order to protect third parties, or when information has been incor-rectly recorded by social workers:

"My records told me I was born out of rape, but when I found my mother she told me that she did know who my father was but wanted to protect him."

DO I REALLY NEED COUNSELLING?

The law requires that people who do not know their birth name and were adopted before November 1975 must be counselled before they are able to obtain this information. Counselling is usually required before information can be given from adoption records.

The counselling process is quite different from that of psychotherapy (with which the term 'counselling' is more often associated). The counsellor is usually a social worker and the aim of the sessions is not to tell you what to do or how to feel, but instead to give you the opportunity to discuss your expectations and consider some of the issues, so that you can be as well equipped as possible to make a success of your search.

We have learned from many people in the adoption circle that finding out information about their origins can have a profound emotional effect. It is understandable that some people resent having to see a counsellor and prefer to handle their own affairs. However, if they wish to come through the process of obtaining information and of finding their birth relatives with as much benefit and as little trauma as possible, then consulting someone who is experienced in these matters can be very helpful.

Alison describes her experience of applying to see her birth records. (Her full account is on pages 71-78.)

"I had absolutely no idea where to start, except that I had been placed through The Children's Society. I rang Headquarters and, to my amazement, they had heard of me, they had my records, they were charming and helpful in the extreme. I don't know what I had expected but this wasn't it. People for whom adoption was not a dirty word. I was shaking from head to toe! My records were on microfilm and unusually complete. I could furnish enough information over the phone for them to locate my file immediately.

But then the bombshell: to progress any further, I had to be counselled. Yuk! In an offhand way I had always pictured people in need of counselling in a somewhat negative light, deficient in some way. My upper lip stiffened. I didn't want to be shut up in some sleezy back room, breathing deeply of the joss-stick-filled smoky air, pouring out my innermost worries to a deeply meaningful do-gooder with a floor-length Indian skirt, a note-pad and a degree in psychology from the 60s. No way, José. For a while I chickened out. A few days later I calmed down. I had also had time to establish that counselling was a legal necessity to progress. I resigned myself, and a counsellor rang me.

A few phone calls later, and I felt very small indeed for having harboured such hasty thoughts about counsellors. I mentally ate large slices of humble pie. When my husband and I went to London to meet my counsellor and to see my records, my theories were further shot to pieces. Sparing her no blushes, she is simply one of the nicest, most approachable, practical and professional people I have ever met. No Indian skirts, no dingy room, not a joss-stick in sight. How naïve I had been."

FEELINGS OF LOSS

All three parties to adoption are usually subject to a loss, and this may play a significant part in the dynamics of tracing.

As a birth mother, you may have suffered a bereavement experience and may have coped with it in a number of ways. Reactions may vary, from mothers who cope by burying the experience right inside themselves so that eventually very little will remind them of it and they will 'get on' with their lives as though it never happened, to mothers who will not give up searching for their child so that it becomes part and parcel of every day of their lives. In between are those who recall at special times such as birthdays and Christmas, and those for whom particular events trigger memories.

As an adoptive parent, you may find that memories are brought back of not being able to have your own child and you may feel that the reunion will mean losing your relationship with your adopted son or daughter.

Adopted people may develop a growing sense of loss as they realize that they are 'different' in not living with the people who conceived them. The sense of loss if brought out into the open can be acknowledged and accepted when a child feels safe in his or her permanent home.

In those cases where a birth parent or a child given up for adoption is found to have died, there may be a double sense of loss. Ruth and Deborah describe how they felt when their search led them to discover that their respective birth mothers had died.

Ruth writes:

"From the papers I was shown by my adoption records counsellor, I read that my alleged father was dead but I suppose I assumed that my mother would be still alive, although I did have doubts.

I pursued one of my brothers rapidly after seeing my counsellor – rather like a bull in a china shop I went straight to the phone. I did not know what to expect, nor had I prepared myself – I played it all by ear. Fortunately Andrew's wife Sheila, whilst suspicious at first, was not hostile to my initial enquiries.

It was from that telephone conversation that I learnt that Emily, my birth mother, was dead. Sheila told me rather as a matter of fact as if talking about a passing acquaintance. I don't believe this was in any way unnatural as I was then still a complete stranger.

I was not surprised to hear that Emily was dead because I suppose over the years I built up a picture of her. I was rejected by adoption and I was doubly rejected by her being dead. It did not feel the same as the death of someone I knew. I don't know whether I mourned for her or not but in a way I felt disappointed and yet again let down. There is no doubt that she held the key to the reason for my adoption and her death has blocked the way to finding out any more.

Her death has caused me irritation. The whole reason of my adoption is still not known. Had she been alive I don't know what I would have expected her to tell me, if anything, and I don't think we would have got on. It would have probably been a disaster.

I feel quite annoyed by her death and the apparent inability to find the answers to my questions.

I sometimes feel pleased that she's dead as I don't know what my reactions would have been or how I would have coped with the situation had she been alive.

I was supposed to go from her life but equally she had managed to go from mine. That may be an element of grief. My sorrow is that I never met the woman. Everyone has a mother good or bad. I never had a mother. I never knew her – I will never know."

Deborah writes:

"All I wanted to do was meet her. It all happened so quickly. One day it was my 18th birthday, a few days later I was sitting in The Children's Society's office receiving information from my adoption file and details about my birth parents: their description, age, occupation, even personality. The first thing I spotted was that my birth mother, Claire, was very young when she had me, which I had always hoped she would be – I don't really know why. I suppose I wanted her to have an excuse to give me up other than that she just didn't want me. I also wanted her to be beautiful. It turned out she was a quiet, pretty blonde. Well, that was the impression I got from her file.

My counsellor gave me advice about tracing and I decided it would be a lot quicker and easier to trace my birth father, David, first as Claire could have married and changed her surname.

We managed to track David down really fast and my counsellor made the first contact (thank goodness). She arranged to call him again in a few days. After speaking to David on this occasion, he told her that Claire was dead. It didn't really hit me until a few days later when my counsellor called back saying it was true. David hadn't known how to say it at first because of my reaction. I can't really explain how I felt when my counsellor told me that she had died the year before at the age of 32. She had committed suicide.

Over the next few days, I found out more and more about Claire from David. The more I found out, the worse I felt. She had been so much like I had wanted her to be. She had also very much wanted to meet me, which I needed to hear. She had been in hospital for severe depression soon after I was adopted. From then on, she was in and out of hospital and she had weight problems, becoming anorexic and only weighing five stone. Claire and David had lived together for nine years after my birth.

My question now is the same as the day I found out she was dead. Why couldn't she have waited? If I had found her eleven months before, things could be different now. But that is a big 'if'.

I have since met Claire's parents, who were over the moon to meet me and had, in fact, tried to trace me. I have also visited Claire's grave and put flowers on it. I have so much informa-

tion about her and photographs, that I feel as though I have met her and knew her. I also have some of her jewellery and clothes and even a tape of her talking, which is amazing.

Claire left behind so many close people who loved her and they are all still so sad. She also left behind someone who never got the chance to get close to her, but will always love her more than anyone will know."

WILL I FALL IN LOVE?

Reunions can bring with them relationships of great intensity and powerful feelings which can be overwhelming and confusing. When meeting a birth relative after many years of separation, you may feel a strong emotional pull to them. For some people it may feel like the love between a child and parent or between a brother and sister; others may view each other as friends. Equally, many will expect to feel an emotional bond but may end up feeling quite distant from one another.

Where there is a strong emotional relationship, you may feel as though you are 'in love'. In some situations a sexual attraction can develop and a sexual relationship can occur. If you have had a reunion and feel this might be a worry for you, do talk it over with someone.

The following account highlights some of the tensions that a new and strong relationship may bring.

"I have known Paul for just over a year now and we get on very well. We even have daughters with the same name.

I don't think it was easy for my husband at first to see me so close to 'another man', and he did experience some jealousy, but

I think that has passed and he and Paul seem to get on well. Both Paul's wife and my husband have been very supportive and given us the time and freedom to get to know each other.

I don't know how Paul feels about our relationship. We find it very difficult to talk about – in fact, we don't talk about it at all. Sometimes we don't seem to know how to react to each other as brother and sister. I know he cares about me and I care a great deal about him, but there is sometimes an 'atmosphere' between us that I can't understand and I certainly can't put into words."

The following example describes an extreme case of sexual attraction between a birth mother and her son.

William was 25 years old when he met his birth mother, Helen. She was just 41 years old and William felt attracted to her immediately. She was young, slim and trendy and did not resemble his image of a mother.

Helen also found William physically attractive; he was so much like William's father at the same age. As the months went by, they became increasingly close to one another. They were in daily contact and exchanged intimate letters.

During a holiday together, they began a sexual relationship. Helen felt guilty and part of her wanted to end the relationship. It had complicated her life. However, she felt ending it would not only destroy any relationship she had had with William, but would also be an act of rejection. She had done this once before and could not bear to do this to William again. She couldn't tell anyone what she had done; she felt remorseful. There was no way out.

Helen committed suicide a year after her relationship began with William.

WHAT ABOUT MY BROTHERS AND SISTERS?

Developing a relationship with either a birth mother or father can be only one aspect of a reunion. Equally important are the relationships that can be formed with brothers and sisters. Sometimes these can be very fulfilling and strong, but equally, jealousies and difficulties may arise. One of the hopes that many adopted people have when they start to trace is that of finding a brother and/or sister. Some will find out this information from their records, but others will have to wait until further contact is made.

There are a number of implications in tracing and meeting siblings. Sometimes it is only the eldest child who has been adopted. When they appear, it can cause jealousy in the child who thought they were the eldest. Sometimes it is the second or third child who was adopted, and they may feel that they were 'singled out' for rejection.

"I went to meet my mother for the first time and although it wasn't planned, I met the two younger girls as well. They behaved very courteously towards me, but were polite rather than friendly.

I went for another weekend to meet Julia, the eldest. I underwent a literal interrogation, which involved a barrage of questions regarding my expectations and motives in renewing contact. I doubt many people would have tolerated the ordeal, but I consented as I felt it was necessary in helping Julia to accept the situation.

I went to stay with Julia for a weekend a month later. We appeared to get on very well, but she seemed intent on using my presence for childminding purposes for her small daughter, while she made arrangements to see friends. We ended up having a blazing row about this, after which we appeared to be reconciled. Julia said she didn't bear grudges – that was in November 1985, and I didn't see or hear from her again until January 1991!

The girls have treated me much like a commodity to be switched on and off as appropriate. They go from being friendly to antagonistic. I've had letters and cards, and last year Julia was so inclined towards me that I was invited to ring her at work any time."

But often, siblings find that their common experience helps to build a relationship which may ultimately be stronger than between the birth mother and child. For example, Alison's reunion with her brothers and sisters has been more positive:

"I have three brothers, two sisters and three step-sisters. It is a very big clan for an 'only child'! Meeting them all has been very easy; we share a sense of humour (weird though it may be!), we like similar things, and have similar views on the world. I have a little brother I never anticipated. I have become particularly close to the sister immediately older than me; my family went to her wedding and she is godmother to my second daughter."

Barbara's experience has been mixed:
"My birth mother's family consists of three daughters, now aged between 30 and 40 years, all adopted by her and her late husband. I felt it would be easy to relate to them because we had all been adopted, but sadly I was quickly disillusioned.

43

Regrettably, it was made clear to me that my turning up was not welcomed by two of my half-sisters. I received a letter before our first meeting saying all sorts of nasty things with the intention of shutting me out. Time has mellowed the situation somewhat, and on the surface everything seems good, but it has left me feeling that I constantly need to be on my guard. I feel it is just a game that is being played in front of my birth mother, and that deep down their feelings are still the same as those expressed in that first letter and that they will never really accept me as a sister. They know that I will not be scared away by what they say or do, and although I prefer their friendship, I have let them know that it is up to them as I am not worried either way.

Fortunately I have a good relationship with my youngest half-sister. We hit it off at the first meeting and have continued to get on well together. I have also made contact by letter and phone with a birth cousin, who sounds nice and is living in the area where I was born. I am looking forward to meeting up with her soon."

ADOPTED PEOPLE'S ACCOUNTS

The following chapter gives accounts from adopted people. Each one is introduced individually and we hope that they will convey some of the emotions, feelings and tensions that can be encountered when searching and having reunions.

Amy

Amy was adopted 35 years ago and primarily wanted only to get more information. It was not her original intention to make contact. She did, but did not feel that she was prepared for the outcome. Her account highlights some of the feelings that touch all parties in the adoption circle and gives some sound advice to people who are thinking about tracing.

"I was adopted as a baby and my adoptive parents were very open with me concerning the circumstances of my adoption. They told me about my origins from as early as I can remember. I have two older brothers, neither of whom are adopted, and they have always known, as have other members of the extended family. As a result, I never felt that need to trace my birth mother. I knew enough about my background to satisfy my curiosity, my adoptive family was my only family and I could not understand the need of other adopted people to trace a parent that had nothing to do with them, meant nothing to them and who they might not actually like if they were to meet. This 'tracing' was definitely not for me and I felt very strongly about this for a long time. Other people thought I was being terribly adult about it all, but in some ways it was a self-preservation exercise. I think I was, and still am to some extent, frightened as to what I might find.

However, when I became pregnant with my first daughter, my attitude changed, partly due to all the medical questions I was asked to which I did not have the answers. But I did nothing further until after my second child was born.

When she was about three, my husband and I considered having a holiday in Ireland. As I knew that my birth mother came from there, I began to think that it might be interesting to visit the area where I might have been brought up. I discussed this with my adoptive parents and they were interested and supportive. In fact, my father was particularly interested, and he suggested that if I ever wanted to see my entire file which The Children's Society had, then I should perhaps do it before it was too late and the file had been destroyed.

The result of all this is that I have made contact with my birth mother by letter. This was the way I wanted it to be and basically the whole tracing business has been on my terms. I did not want physical contact with my birth mother because I felt quite strongly that the privacy of my mother should be preserved. After all, it is quite likely that no one in her family ever knew of my existence, and what right have I to upset that position? Furthermore, for all I knew, my mother might have married and might never have told her husband of my existence. What pain it might cause her for me suddenly to turn up out of the blue.

However, once I discovered that she was not married, I decided that the best way for me to proceed was to write her a letter telling her a little about me and sending her a photograph of myself and my family. I explained that I did not want to cause any more distress than was absolutely unavoidable and that I did not intend to correspond with her on a regular basis. I really just wanted her to know that everything had turned out for the best.

What I did not prepare myself for, however, was the possibility that she might not want to make any contact with me by acknowledging my letter. As I said before, everything had been done on my terms and I had not really considered the fact that she might not be overjoyed to hear from me. Everything was alright when I was in the driving seat, but all of a sudden I wasn't and that was quite difficult to deal with.

I have to be honest and say that I was not prepared for the feeling of rejection which I felt, but time has passed now and I have come to terms with it. After all, my birth mother is quite entitled to deal with this situation in her own way, which may not correspond with the way I wanted to deal with the matter.

I should also add that tracing can create difficulties within your own immediate family. My husband was not at all keen that I embark on an albeit limited tracing exercise. He felt that it would end up causing me and other family members pain unnecessarily. In the end, he agreed that it was up to me and was supportive. Perhaps he was right about the pain.

On a more positive note, the whole exercise has been very satisfying in that I have managed to obtain a photograph of my birth mother, which is lovely to have, and I found out some facts about my background that I did not already know. I feel now that I have found out as much as there is to know so that I shall be able to satisfy my own children's curiosity when they get older.

I do feel strongly that tracing is a very complex business and it is a generalization to say that all adopted people have a burning desire to discover their real family. My real and only family is my adoptive family and I have no interest in creating another family. Also, when my birth mother gave me up for adoption, she did so in the knowledge that it was in absolute confidence. What right do I have suddenly to reappear after all these years and expect her to form part of my life? She is a complete stranger to me and I to her. I also do not want to hurt her by digging up the past which she may well have tried to forget or tried to block out all these years. The feelings of the birth mother must be considered carefully before embarking on the tracing process. Otherwise, it becomes a selfish, one-sided, ill-considered venture."

Rebecca

Rebecca has found both her birth father and mother. She describes how she did this and how she is unable to tell her adoptive parents.

"I was always aware that I was adopted. My parents told me as early as I can remember that my 'proper' mother and father did not have a home ready for me. (In my youthful innocence I took this to mean that the curtains were not yet up or there still remained some decorating to do!)

As I reached my teens, and particularly around the age of 14, I encountered all the usual emotional problems associated with growing into adulthood – not least the sense of 'who am I?' and 'why am I here?' (remember?!) Added to this though was a sense of not belonging, and my awkward feelings towards my parents I put down to being adopted (whilst other friends were wishing they were!).

I knew that I wanted to discover more about my 'roots' although part of me felt guilty because my adoptive parents had given me such a wonderful home and I could not have wished for a more stable and loving upbringing. What I found hardest to cope with was seeing other friends who actually looked like their parents and their brothers and sisters (both my brothers are adopted too).

When I was 18, I duly applied for my original birth certificate and after initial counselling was informed that my original name was Catherine. This was quite a strange experience, not only because I had always liked that name, but also because it didn't seem like 'me' on that piece of paper. After all, I am called Rebecca and one's name is so much part of one's identity.

It was peculiar to see my birth mother's name and to have confirmed the real reason for being adopted (i.e. no mention of my father on the birth certificate).

Now knowing my name as I was registered at birth, I then wrote to The Children's Society to see if they had any records of my Adoption Order. For some reason, I didn't expect them still to have files on me and was quite shocked to receive a letter soon after telling me all about my pre-adoption identity. It told me my weight at birth, the hospital where I was born, how old my mother was, who my father was, how they met, why they never married and other pieces of information that others take for granted. The most amazing fact was that they met at a Young Communists' Club!

There were addresses on the letter, but these were so out of date that I didn't expect tracing to be an easy job. Also, I felt that I had found as much as I wanted, or at least as much as I could assimilate in one go.

The story continues seven years later at the age of 25, when the desire to find the people who I look like had still not died away.

I went to the Society's Headquarters, where I met a counsellor. He was able to give me a lot more information regarding my adoption, including reports of me as a baby and detailed records of my parents' history and background. He also prepared me for a great shock – my mother had changed her mind at the eleventh hour and decided not to give me up, despite my having been on trial with my adoptive parents for three months. My adoptive parents (hereafter referred to as my parents as, let's fact it, they truly are!) never found this out. Obviously my mother, Jenny, relented in time, otherwise my life would have been so different.

My next step was St Catherine's House where I prepared to pitch up tent for the week in order to trace Jenny's marriage entry.

I began looking in volumes from 1967 – two years after my birth, as I thought this would be the earliest time she might have considered marrying. After only two volumes (ten minutes), I found what I was looking for. Jenny had married at the age of 19 – but to a Mr Smith! My hopes of tracing her last known address by looking up the birth of her latest child were dashed. There were thousands of Smiths in each volume and I had no idea what year to look under or the names of any of her children.

I decided to be pessimistic and hoped she had got divorced! Nevertheless, I ordered a copy of the marriage certificate which arrived a few weeks later. From that I was able to get her address at the time of marriage (albeit 23 years out of date) and also her husband's address at that time. It was a shot in the dark, but I rang (yes, rang) her husband's parents' address and unbelievably they still lived there. From then on it was straightforward. Ashamedly, I gave some yarn about being a long lost friend of Jenny's ex-husband and I was given all the information I needed. Yes, they were divorced – about 12 years ago, but they were still in touch because of the children. I was given Jenny's new name since her second marriage and her address!

Immediately I wrote, although very anxious that I would not give her too great a shock or disrupt her family. The next day, I returned from work to find a tearful message on my answerphone. "Rebecca – it's Jenny. I got your letter today and I want you to know that there hasn't been a day gone by that I haven't thought of you."

I rang her up at once and we cried and spoke for over an hour! I couldn't believe how easy it was to get on with her. She has a very similar sense of humour (warped!) and a fairly laid-back approach to life despite two marriages and never having forgiven herself for giving me up (although she does now).

She sent me some photos of herself – one when she was pregnant with me. There is a definite likeness. (I mean in looks, not pregnancy!) Jenny was afraid I would not like her if I met her, but I knew from our phone calls and letters that we would get on. I think she felt that I might somehow resent her for giving me away – or worse still, be extremely grateful that she did.

I arranged to drive down to the south coast to visit her at her home. On the day, I was extremely nervous and it was only the encouragement and support of my friend who accompanied me that got me to drive down Jenny's road.

It was a story book reunion. Jenny met me at the door and we just hugged each other and cried, and then wondered if our mascara had smudged. At first it was rather emotional and we found it hard to find anything to say, but after seeing a photo album with all my family contained therein, things relaxed. We spent a lovely day together. We kept staring at each other. I had come face to face with someone with my green eyes, straight 'boring brown' hair and fingers that bent back on double joints – weird after 25 years! When I left, I felt a sense of grief. I'd spent so long wondering about this person and now I had to leave her again.

Since then we have kept in touch. She managed to trace my father who lives quite near me! I also met him and his family. (My two half-brothers felt a little awkward, being teenagers and only having recently found out about me, but were friendly enough.)

My father is musical, which is interesting, as that is my profession. But as both my (adoptive) parents are professional musicians, who is to know what's hereditary and what's environment?

I know I have been very lucky in my experiences and realize it does not always work out for people. However, I would say that if the desire to trace your roots is there, it is unlikely to go away and my advice would be 'go for it!' I don't feel particularly different for having met my birth parents. In fact, I rarely think about it now. I suppose it just satisfied my curiosity, and although I have not felt able to tell my adoptive parents yet, it has not changed my feelings towards them in any way. They are the people who have made me what I am and it is to them that I owe my gratitude."

David

David's decision to search for his birth mother followed the death of his adoptive parents and the break-up of his marriage. His account describes the way in which expectations do not always become a reality and that this is something all parties have to come to terms with.

"In order to find out more information about my birth mother, I had to be seen by a counsellor. We talked over the information she had managed to obtain. I was amazed to find that so much information could be found about events over 40 years ago. I found this meeting very emotional but I was very pleased to know so much more. I found out that I had a half-brother and that my mother was divorced as a result of my appearance on the scene. My real father was a soldier my mother had met only briefly.

The existence of my half-brother gave me great hope about finding more information, as it was very likely that he would be alive now (I could not be certain about my mother who would be about 71 years old).

My research eventually yielded the marriage certificate of my half-brother's son. His marriage had taken place only a few years previously, so I was hopeful of being able to trace him with such recent information. After more searching, I managed to find the telephone number of the parents of my half-brother's daughter-in-law. At this point I had a lot of emotional feelings – I wanted to find out more; I knew that I had no right to interfere and my relatives must be allowed to say they were not interested; I did not want to be told 'not interested'!

It was about seven p.m. when I rang my counsellor to tell her I had got as far as getting the phone number. She said she would ring the number for me and see what she could find out. I expected her to do this the following day – I was absolutely amazed when she rang back about an hour later to say that she had actually spoken to my birth mother!

At first my mother was so taken aback that she said to my counsellor that she didn't want to know – it was a thing in the distant past and she did not want to think about that now. However, my counsellor was obviously an expert in these matters and persuaded my mother to allow me to contact her.

I rang my mother after a few moments hesitation – we spoke on the phone for about two and a half hours. I was absolutely overwhelmed by the experience. We agreed to meet on the following Saturday.

I was quite excited about the meeting and wondered if I would instinctively recognize my mother. I did not. In fact we nearly missed one another because I was looking for a lady on her own and, as I now know often happens, my mother had struck up a conversation with some strangers in the hotel. She was telling them how amazing it was that she was meeting her son for the first time in 45 years.

My mother did not look anything like I expected – although I don't know what I was expecting. She is very different from my adoptive mother. I expected her to be taller, especially because she has a very posh voice and sounded very grand on the phone. She is very small but makes a point of always being immaculately dressed. My adoptive mother was definitely more working class and my birth mother is definitely more middle class. My adoptive mother was not ambitious and seemed to be quite content as a housewife. My birth mother regrets not being able to achieve some of the career goals that she had in the past. Her second husband died some ten years ago.

Because of my birth and my mother's divorce from her first husband at that time, my half-brother went with his father to Scotland and was kept out of touch with his mother. My mother did not really have contact with him until he was about 27 and his wife encouraged him to get in touch. My mother is always saying how well she copes on her own, but I think she is a bit lonely. She has a sister who lives in the same village. They regularly see one another but my mother has always felt she is in second place to her sister.

My mother also has an aunt and uncle living in the village. Aunty is 98 but still going strong and so is Uncle. At first my mother did not tell them about me but she has done now. I am sure she felt a bit ashamed of becoming pregnant from a brief fling with a soldier. When we first met, my mother said she wasn't going to tell her sister about me just yet. However, on that first Saturday we did go and see her. I suspect my mother wanted her sister to see me to prove it was all real.

I have kept in touch with my mother and will continue to do so. She has come to visit us for a weekend and we have taken her to France for a short break (she had never been abroad before).

I am not certain whether I will ever become close to my mother, it would need more regular contact I think. I am pleased that I have found her as it seems to give me a positive link with the past which previously I was missing."

Elizabeth

The following was written by Elizabeth, who is of mixed parentage and was adopted by a white family. Her account highlights some of the problems and conflicting emotions that transracial adoption may bring.

I was brought up in a predominantly white middle-class area. I had the best childhood I can ever imagine possible. As a child, the fact of being brought up in a white family and community didn't worry me at all. I suppose that I wasn't aware that I was any different from my family. I knew I was a different colour, of course, but I didn't feel any different. In fact I looked pretty much just like a tanned European child.

When I was about eight or nine, my skin got noticeably darker and my hair went brown from its fair colour. Then at puberty, my hair turned frizzy and that was probably the worst thing. I just felt different from everybody else and I got a real complex about being black. I still didn't feel black but everybody at secondary school used to tell me I was a 'Paki' or a 'wog'. I felt very isolated. I didn't feel I could go to my parents and talk to them about it, and if I did, they really didn't know how to respond.

So as far as I was concerned, it was bad to be black and I had nobody to tell me any different. I had no other role model to show me that there was nothing wrong with it. All the time people made me feel that 'you're not one of us'. But if you're not one of the people you've grown up with, there are no other role models, you're a nobody. So I grew up feeling bad about myself.

Even now at the age of 20, I still have a residue of feeling, almost like a racist feeling, that it's bad to be black. And it's very hard to come to terms with being, in a way, racist against yourself. I think it would have been easier if my parents had had a clearer understanding of how they saw me before they adopted me. But they had no counselling about it. As far as they were concerned, I was their child and I was going to fit in with the rest of their family and everyone around them. I think it would have helped me a lot even if they had just referred to the term 'mixed-race' or 'coloured' or something. I once asked my Dad when I was about 16 how he saw me – was I black or white or what? He said, "You're white of course". But I'm not white, I'm a bit of both, and I still don't know what to call myself.

My family is very much white-orientated, and they have given me a very strong British identity. That's great, but I have no personal identity that relates to my colour. Instead, that is something that I'm only now finding for myself. If somebody had counselled my parents and had told them what they might expect, what problems might arise, they would have been more prepared and perhaps they would have talked to me about it more.

I wish my parents had questioned more when they adopted me and had asked for more information. If they had known that there would be a possibility that I might trace then perhaps they would have queried the ambiguities and inadequacies of the information they were given. It's always easy with hindsight to say what people should have done. I'm not criticizing my parents.

One of the main problems was my hair. I had nice curly 'European' hair until I was about 12 or 13. Then it suddenly went frizzy. My mother still used to take me to the hairdresser's and because she didn't know what to do with it, she basically cut the lot off. It was as if she was saying, let's get rid of that, it's not very nice. And I went to a hairdresser who told me she wouldn't cut my hair. "We don't do your sort here," she told me.

If my parents had considered the fact that, as they had a mixed-race child, I was quite probably going to have Afro hair, then they might have thought that I would need different care for my hair. Something as simple as taking me along to a hairdresser who would have known what to do with my hair would have made a huge difference.

I didn't know very much about my birth family. My parents always told me I was adopted, but they told me a nice little story about how my Mum and Dad couldn't look after me. But when I was about seven or eight, I realized that perhaps this wasn't quite the full story and I started wondering what had actually happened.

It took me a year to ask my Mum whether my birth parents had been married because I was so scared to bring the whole thing up with her. She told me that they weren't, and I wanted to know why. The only information that I had was my birth mother's age, name and very vague information about what she looked like, including the fact that she was white. It could have been anybody.

My father was just a man with black curly hair, brown skin, brown eyes, 5'7", which describes a lot of people. It said on my adoption form that he was part Afro-Caribbean, but I didn't have that information until I was about 15 or 16 and I'd spent three years looking for it. I couldn't bring myself to ask my parents for it.

I think that it was because the information was so sketchy that my birth parents were always on my mind. Questions kept going round and round in my head: what are they like? who are they? I knew that unless I found out who they were or at least got some information, I would never be comfortable.

But even more important was the fact that I knew so little about my ethnic origins. People ask where you are from and the answer 'I don't know' is not good enough. Although I wanted to meet my birth parents, what I really wanted was to fill in all the missing blanks for me: where I came from, my origins, why I was adopted, why my parents weren't together, what happened.

When I got more information about my birth parents, I found out that my Dad wasn't from where I had originally been told he was from. Although first of all I just wanted to find out where I came from, once I'd seen the information and found out that I had two sisters – I never knew that I had sisters – and that they both had names, suddenly they were people, they were real. When I saw my birth parents' signatures, they were no longer abstract. They had handwriting, they had addresses they used to live at.

I had always wanted to find my mother just to let her know that I was alright and happy. I never thought I would carry on seeing her. I wanted to meet my father more out of curiosity, to see what he looked like.

I have now met both of them. Having met my father, I feel that I have some sort of peace about my identity, some sense of my Caribbean half. Even though I still have a lot of problems about it and am still not sure what to call myself, I do at least take pride in being mixed-race. I have a black family and they're real people. I tasted West Indian food for the first time last year and I also met my sisters. They were quite astonished that I didn't know what to do with my hair when I was

18 years old and my sister has put hair extensions in for me. Thanks to them, I am happier with looking after my hair and I can take a sort of pride in the way I look.

The most difficult thing – and I don't think it makes any difference whether it's a white parent or a black parent – is meeting somebody who you know is your mother or your father and yet they are complete strangers. And even though you know logically that there is no reason why you should feel anything for them, by the simple fact that you know that they are your parents, you feel there should be something there. You are strangers and yet you are not strangers. If you met them and you didn't know they were your parents you might never bother to talk to them. But you have to talk to them, and you feel that you have to make it work even if it's just for one meeting.

I don't think I was really equipped for a reunion at all. No matter how much talking you do beforehand, how much counselling you have, how you might mull over what might happen, when it comes down to it, everything depends on who the person is you're meeting.

In fact, after I had met my birth father for the first time, I went home and thought 'what have I done?' I felt that I had made a big mistake that I was going to regret for a long time. Not knowing is safe. However much you want to know, once you've made that step you can't go back. It's a whole new life and I feel that the two are completely different.

I still feel they're different. I have my life with my adoptive parents and if I go and visit my birth father I'm stepping into another world. It's almost as though I have to be a different person with them. To a certain extent I still have to watch what I say, making sure that when I talk about my Mum and Dad I refer to them as my 'adoptive parents'. I don't think that I was prepared for that.

My adoptive father is a policeman. He is very pro-British and has a strong British identity. My birth father's family would sometimes be quite racist about white people and had very negative views about the police – they were just 'racist pigs'. I felt a real pull between my adoptive family, everything I was used to, the loyalty I felt to them, and this new part of me, my black side, my black family. I almost felt torn apart because I wanted to experience black culture, but I was already defending my life with my adoptive family. I feel that I am in the middle and I am probably biased to the white side of me. That's difficult because when you're mixed-race, you're neither one thing nor the other.

Your colour shouldn't make any difference, but it does. It's not just the colour, it's the culture and people saying "Do you want some of this?" and describing some food and giving it a name and you don't have a clue what it is. Even now, I still feel quite lost. I found meeting my birth mother a lot easier. I felt more attuned to her.

I don't think I'll ever be as happy with my identity and self-image as if I had been brought up with a clear picture of it. Normally people don't have to sort it out, but I'm always questioning it. I think because I live in a white family and nearly all of my friends are white, it is difficult sometimes to have to jump between one world and another. Now that I have found my birth family and met them, in many ways I just want to carry on as normal.

Karen

This account was written by Karen who decided not to embark on a search for information relating to her origins until her adoptive parents had died. Karen's experience highlights some of the positive and negative emotions reunions can bring.

"It is now almost a year since I met my birth mother for the first time after 45 years. No amount of counselling can really prepare one for that first reunion. You do not have an automatic right to be accepted, or even liked, just because you were born out of your mother's womb. Even if she wants to accept you she might be scared or ashamed to admit it to her family for fear she might be rejected by them, so their reactions would have a considerable bearing on the success or otherwise of this reunion.

I thought I was strong enough to handle rejection, but luckily I didn't have to put it to the test. The longest two weeks of my life were waiting for a reply from the introductory letter. Yes, she wanted to see me, but didn't know how to tell her family. She was going to introduce me as one of the hundred or more foster children she had taken care of in the last 30 years of her working life. I was bitter at this. There was a part of me that was incomplete. To make me whole, I needed recognition, total acceptance by her. I felt, maybe selfishly, that it was a small price to pay for all those lost years. I meant her no harm. I had nothing to give her but my love and reassurance that I understood that she had no choice but to give me away and that I didn't blame her at all. I thanked her for the way my life had turned out and if she had as much love and happiness in her lifetime as I had in mine, then she had nothing to reproach herself for.

She said that she was jealous of my adoptive mother and thanked her by name. I was really proud of my adoptive parents at that moment, and still feel quite emotional when I think back to that time. I wish in my heart that my adoptive parents could be here now so I could give them a hug and tell them I love them so much, and that my searching out my birth mother has made no difference to the way I feel for them. Still, that is not to be. If they were still alive, I wouldn't be writing this now. I know I wouldn't have had the strength to go through with my search, as I feel it would have given them too much pain.

Great courage is needed for everyone in the triangle of birth mother, adoptive parents and adoptee when you decide to go in search of your origins. The same courage as it took my birth mother, not only to accept me back in her life, but also to give me full recognition in her family. You can't imagine how wonderful that moment felt. I was whole again, I belonged!

Her family consists of three daughters, now aged between 30 and 40 years, all adopted by her and her late husband. I felt it would be easy to relate to them because we had all been adopted, but sadly I was quickly disillusioned. Regrettably, it was made clear to me that my turning up was not welcomed by two of my half sisters. I received a letter before our first meeting saying all sorts of nasty things with the intention of shutting me out. Time has mellowed the situation somewhat and on the surface everything seems good, but it has left me feeling that I constantly need to be on my guard. I feel it is just a game that is being played in front of my birth mother and that deep down their feelings are still the same as those expressed in that first letter and that they will never really accept me as a sister. They know that I will not be scared away by what they say or do, and although I prefer their friendship, I have let them know that it is up to them as I am not worried either way. Maybe in time we will be able to build up something more genuine. Fortunately I have a good relationship with my youngest half-sister. We hit it off at the first meeting and have continued to get on well together.

I have made contact by letter and phone with a birth cousin who sounds nice and is living in the area I was born in, and I am looking forward to meeting with her soon. She is very close to one of the elder sisters and so our meeting should be quite interesting. I am also interested in finding my birth father. This is proving to be next to impossible, as unfortunately I do not have enough information about him and so far all I have met with is a brick wall. I live in hope, although I feel time is fast running out.

In the meantime, my birth mother and I are enjoying each other's company. I visit once a month and we had a really special first Christmas together when I managed to get her to come down to stay with me. She liked her stay so much she wants to come down again in the summer; that's some recommendation and I feel good about that. It was clear on that first meeting that she had given up the will to live. My finding her has given her back that will, and I am overjoyed. Selfishly, I want to have her around for many more years. We have so much to learn about each other – a whole lifetime.

My husband Neil is still very much in my life, and is offering me endless support. He devoted many hours in helping me with my searching. It became an obsession with me, and Neil took it all in his stride. He was caught up in my emotions and we spent endless hours trying to make sense of them. I don't think he can truly understand my needs to follow this road. Who can, who hasn't been adopted? It's hard enough for those of us who have.

My adoptive father was Neil's uncle. Neil knew from the beginning that I was adopted and has accepted always that I am part of his family. That was until I started my search for my origins. He found it difficult to embrace my birth family as part of his family and saw himself as very much an outsider. I was terribly upset by this. I felt he was shutting me out of his life. He is very much a part of my family and it took a lot of reassurance for him to accept that. He now feels that he belongs too, and that makes us both feel good."

Mark

Mark contacted The Children's Society when he was 23 years old. After receiving information from this records, he made a search of the Marriage Indexes at St Catherine's House and discovered that his birth parents had married. He was excited and thought that his contact with them would be welcomed. He was not prepared for the rejection which initially followed.

I have always known that I was adopted; entwined with this knowledge was the wish to meet my genetic parents.

Taking the big step of making contact is not an easy one. I waited until I was absolutely certain that I wanted to know these people for the rest of my life. Once you've spoken or met you will always know them, even if you don't keep in touch.

In May of 1992 I know the time had come, and I rang The Children's Society and eventually I spoke to a counsellor and arranged a counselling session.

My counsellor was very open, and listened to everything objectively. I must stress here that up until then, being rejected by one or both of my parents was something I thought would never happen to me, it only happened to other people. My counsellor made me more aware of the strong chance of it happening, without making me lose hope. For once, I had to be pessimistic, expect the worst, and anything good is a bonus.

I saw my adoption records, learnt my mother's name and all of her family and, surprisingly, I learnt the same details about my father. I had not expected to see those, and was elated to know about him. The people who I had imagined all my life now had names, hobbies, education records - a life. Fortunately, there were no nasty circumstances, and on this basis I decided to go ahead and trace.

I went to St Catherine's House to see if there were any registrations of marriage or children. I found that they had married each other and that I had a young brother. I was absolutely elated. I had always hoped that everything had worked out well for them and secretly wished that they had married. On discovering this, all ideas of rejection by them went out of my head, and I got very excited about meeting them and my young brother. From electoral rolls I found that my uncle lived at the same address and my counsellor wrote via him to my parents Tim and Rita.

We heard nothing, so some weeks later we wrote again, thinking that the first letter might not have reached them. A couple of days later Rita rang my counsellor who related this message to me that evening. Rita said that although she wanted me to be happy, I was not to spend my life looking for them as the decision made in 1968 still stood firm. I couldn't take this at first. The TV was on, I sat in front of it watching a programme about starving children in Romania whose parents had deserted them.

I ran out of the flat and ran for a mile or so, crying.

I took the next day off work, sat on the floor all day wondering why and crying. I got it out of my system but still couldn't understand it. I have never felt rejected before.

Rita rang my counsellor a few days later to ask how I'd taken the news. On hearing my counsellor's reply, she promised to ring back another time. She rang back the next day. The thing to remember here is that having had all my hopes crushed, I had to sustain the 'no expectations' theory, even though I knew things were changing. She said that they didn't want to ruin my life and, on that basis, would meet me. I was pleased and not pleased, as I wanted them to meet me because they wanted to and not because they felt they should. However, I took this as my only chance, agreed to let my counsellor pass on my phone number and my name and within a week, I had spoken to Tim.

We arranged to meet six weeks later, and I spoke to him a couple of times on the phone. Once he became 'real' I got serious cold feet, but knew I couldn't go back now. Rita phoned a couple of weeks before we met, and explained that their reservations were centred around Andrew, their son, as they hadn't told him about me. We were both glad to have spoken as it made a little bridge before meeting.

The onslaught of emotion that followed that meeting was at times totally consuming, and has only recently subsided. This has been happiest time of my life. Being re-united with them has enabled me to find everything I wanted to.

In the first few days after the meeting, Rita and I talked incessantly over the phone. We quickly discovered all our similarities, and I gradually started putting all the missing links into place. This is not, as I am still learning, a rapid process.

All of us have been flung into an emotional whirlpool and only now, almost a year on, are we starting to surface.

When I learnt of the situation at the time of my birth and subsequent days spent together, it suddenly hit me that these people were parents – they ceased to be people whose names I knew, they were my flesh and blood. Here I was entering dangerous ground. My adoptive parents were suddenly appearing unnatural to me and the common links found with Tim and Rita are very natural. If I hadn't realized this I could quite easily have 'forgotten' my other parents, but I now classify them all as 'my parents'. This is very important to establish.

In those initial few weeks, we were all totally consumed with the situation. We would speak every day. It was a need, not a necessity, and we would meet whenever we could, even if it was just for an hour or so. I remember that each time they left I was scared of never seeing them again. This comes from my massive fear of rejection which I, and many other adoptees I have spoken to, have. Because of this fear, I went out of my way to avoid my problems or, I suppose, let them see the 'real me', although they were unaware that they were being duped. I had to construct some sort of protective barrier – which, with trust, gradually came down.

I have often wondered what would have happened if the meeting had been a disaster. Would we have stayed in touch? The truth is that I don't know, but as time gone on, I find that all of us are different people from the ones that met last year. So whatever the outcome of a meeting, perseverance is a must, as so much common ground will be reached later.

It must be said that they, unbeknown to me, were just as frightened of me turning up, getting the information I needed and disappearing. The build-up to making the decision to contact, and on contact and prior to meeting, is absolutely fraught with fear. You don't know what they're thinking and *vice versa*. This is sometimes enough to put people off, but it isn't a valid reason.

I spent the first four months of this relationship in utter disbelief and astonishment. I could neither take in nor deal with the emotional wrangle that followed the meeting, that followed each phone call, that kept me awake night after night wondering about it all. I was very confused and absolutely elated all in one.

I think this is when you need someone to talk to the most. My counsellor was always on the end of the phone, should I ever need to talk. The experience is so upheaving that at times I thought I would explode if I didn't talk.

The benefits to all of us have been vast. On a personal level, I am now much more self-assured because I now know why I'm like I am. The time I spent with my family is very precious, and the relationship is now settling down into some sort of 'normality'. I no longer feel as if I'm visiting, but rather that I'm going home – and as for what took place in 1968? I think every case is different, mine is not one of resentment, bitterness or hurt but simply a wish that things had been different, that I hadn't had to be adopted, and my only regret is that I didn't make contact sooner. From now on, the way forward is to put the adoption behind us. We've discussed it at length, we will never forget it but just let it rest, appreciate our time together as a close and loving reunited family.

Vanessa

Vanessa was not adopted until she was five years old. She lived with her birth mother and step-father until she was taken into care, and has no memories of her time with them. She was removed from her birth mother due to cruelty and neglect. Vanessa's adoption was a happy one and it was not until her adoptive parents died that she felt the need to search for her original family.

I first decided to look for my birth mother when my husband (who was in the army) was posted back to London from Gibraltar. I realized that our new home was only about three miles from where my birth mother had lived and could still be living. As both my adoptive parents had died, I decided to look for my mother.

I started by writing to The Children's Society in 1988. My counsellor was so helpful, kind and very understanding, and I was able to contact him any time I felt I needed help and support. He provided me with a lot of paperwork and information which helped to start my search.

I wrote to NORCAP and was put onto their computer. In the meantime, unbeknown to me, a half-brother had also been told to do the same thing. My half-brother, Andrew, had been searching for me for about 15 years, even employing a private detective in desperation. Andrew actually found an older sister living in Liverpool. She told me later that when Andrew got in touch with her he believed that Teresa, my sister, was me and it was quite a while before he would believe that she was not. He was apparently very disappointed and had a very strained relationship with Teresa, from what she has told me.

I went on holiday to Gibraltar in 1989 and when I returned I had a letter waiting for me from NORCAP stating that they thought they had found a sister in Liverpool which was a surprise because I thought I only had a brother, from the paperwork I had in my possession. After a few weeks of checking from NORCAP, they phoned me at work and said that this sister would like to contact me and could they give her my home phone number, which I agreed to.

I had a phone call the next evening. It felt so strange to be talking to this lady. Teresa told me that our mother had died from cancer in the early sixties at the age of about 42. She was buried in a pauper's grave near Edgware, I believe. I talked to Teresa for over an hour and she told me that in all there are five children, three of us with different fathers: Teresa, the eldest, in her fifties, myself 44, Andrew 39, then brother Stuart and sister Margaret both in their early thirties. Teresa asked me if I would like Andrew to get in touch with me as he had been searching for me for so long, but she did warn me that he did seem somewhat strange.

Andrew phoned me a couple of nights later, and we had a very strained conversation for about an hour. He kept asking me if I still had my curly blonde hair, which obviously I haven't. He told me that he was punished and abused when he was small, the same as I was by my step-father, Andrew's father. He told me that he was blamed for the fact that I was taken away from the house for adoption and he had lived with that all his life. He told me about the things that used to happen to myself and him which I honestly cannot remember any of. I know this to be true, as I spoke to an aunt of Andrew's later who told me what used to go on.

My husband and I made arrangements to meet Andrew one Saturday afternoon. Needless to say, I was very apprehensive. Andrew was very withdrawn, he lived in a rundown bedsit, was divorced and had had a couple of breakdowns in the last few years. It was a very strange meeting and to both of us somewhat disappointing as I wasn't the little girl with blonde curly hair that he remembered when I left the house all those years ago. I felt I could not get close to him – there seemed to be a wall between us.

After the meeting, I phoned him a couple of times after he had had time to think about our meeting and he said that he really wasn't interested in keeping in touch. When I phoned a few months later to see if he had changed his mind, somebody came on the line and said that he had moved out and they did not know where he had gone. We have not been in touch since – he has completely disappeared. He made me feel guilty about the way he felt towards me, as I did not live up to his expectations.

Both Teresa and Andrew told me that there was another brother and sister but it seems they did not want to know at first when all this came to light, especially my brother, Stuart.

I made a trip up to Liverpool to meet Teresa at her home and what a lovely surprise I got – a lovely, warm, bright, red-haired lady, very friendly and, like me, eager to keep this relationship going. What a difference to Andrew. I couldn't believe the complete opposites. Teresa also had a very hard time. Her adoptive mother told her, not that long ago, that our mother had tried to smother her with a pillow when she was a baby. Luckily for Teresa, a neighbour came in and found her. She was also taken away from our mother. Both Teresa and I still keep in touch and phone when we can.

Out of the blue last year, I had a phone call from Stuart. It seems he had had a change of heart about getting in touch with us all and had phoned Teresa for my phone number. She had phoned to tell me that he would be getting in touch, but it was quite a shock when he did phone. He lived fairly close by with his wife and family of four. Again, we got on really well and made arrangements to meet at his house. My husband and I were made very welcome and all my apprehension disappeared, especially after the meeting with Andrew. Stuart and his family came over to us on several occasions. We have the same sense of humour and temperament. He has moved house recently, so I have not heard from him for a while. I just hope he will be in touch again. His sister, Margaret, has still not been in touch.

To sum up my feelings towards all this and my new-found family, I must say I'm not over-excited, although I should be, but I'm glad I've met my relatives. I'm disappointed that I never knew my mother, but from what I've been told about the way we were all treated by her, perhaps it's just as well. I achieved what I set out to do and I'm quite happy and satisfied with the outcome."

Alison

Alison's account describes what made her search, the effects it had on her family – both adoptive and birth – and how she feels two years later.

I decided to find out about my past when I was 28. The deciding factor was, of all things, a discussion programme one morning on adoption.

Adopted at the age of eight months, I was brought up as the only child of older parents. The adoption itself, to their credit, never caused me any problems. I always knew I was adopted and they answered my questions openly and fairly. In theory, the placement was extremely successful. There were very few problems until I hit adolescence, whereupon my parents and I could agree on nothing, although I figured this was pretty much par for the course, adopted or not. The battles were continuous and ferocious; during this time I was determined to find out about my past as soon as I reached 18 and announced so frequently.

It occurred to me gradually, however, that I was hurting my adoptive parents very deeply. So when I was 18, I chickened out and the plan changed – I would find my birth family when I left home, without having to tell my adoptive parents and hurt them. That sounded nicer. When I finally got away from home and when it boiled down to it, I was afraid to go looking for my birth family. I wasn't secure enough in myself. So maybe I would look them up when I was married and settled. Maybe when I had kids, maybe on the twelfth of never. After all, who needed two mothers anyway, when I had enough trouble with one! And so the plan got shelved, although just occasionally in quiet moments I would take it down, dust and polish it, and then put it back as before.

They say that for an adoptee who has no memory of their birth family, meeting your first offspring and therefore your first 'blood relative' is a very moving experience. Imagine my total disbelief then, when on the appointed day my 'lump' turned out to be a clone of my husband. Was I doomed never to meet anyone who looked like me? Had I truly been beamed in from origins on Mars? Delighted with my daughter though I was, I had not been prepared for how disappointed I could be too.

Six months later, I happened to turn the telly on and caught the start of a discussion programme on adoption and my ears pricked up. The next half-hour or so changed my life forever. There in front of me was a studio full of parents who had given their children up for adoption. I was glued. I scoured all the faces. I listened to all the stories. Could my mother possibly be there? I didn't see, as I had dreaded, cold and hard-faced individuals who had glibly given their children away. I saw tears and heartache and grief from loving parents who had been parted from their children by circumstance and opinion. I cried too.

Then I heard one mother say, "30 years ago I gave up my son in the belief that I was doing the very best I could for him. But for 30 years I have been haunted by the memory of his little face as they took him away, tormented by the doubt that I did the right thing. If I had murdered him 30 years ago, my sentence would be over by now. But what I did then condemned me to a sentence that will never end." I cried with her. I looked across at my little daughter who at six months was the same age I had been when I was given up, and it dawned on me how much my mother must have gone through to do what she believed was best. I would move heaven and earth not to part with my baby; could my mother be so very different from me?

Suddenly I was down a deep well of emotions I had not experienced before. The horror of giving up my own child had previously been something I could not imagine. Surely you could never forget your child? The people on the programme admitted they were there in the faint hope that their child might be watching and contact them. Very few other legal options were open to them. What sort of life, through their own best intentions, were these people condemned to? I decided it was the time to take the old plan off the shelf and dust it off for good. I would establish some facts and unless the omens were very bad indeed, try to make contact. I felt that my mother deserved to know, if nothing else, that I was alive, healthy, happy and perfectly at peace with what she did. As her child, I decided to gamble on her needs and reactions being similar to mine; and I would want to know what had happened to my child.

I had absolutely no idea where to start, except that I had been placed through The Children's Society. I rang Headquarters and to my amazement, they had heard of me, they had my records, they were charming and helpful in the extreme. I don't know what I had expected but this wasn't it. People for whom adoption was not a dirty word – I was shaking from head to toe! My records were on microfilm and unusually complete. I could furnish enough information over the phone for them to locate my file immediately. But then the bombshell: to progress any further, I had to be counselled. Yuk! In an off-hand way I had always pictured people in need of counselling in a somewhat negative light, deficient in some way. My upper lip stiffened. I didn't want to be shut up in some sleezy back room, breathing deeply of the joss-stick-filled smoky air, pouring out my innermost worries to a deeply meaningful do-gooder with a floor-length Indian skirt, a note-pad and a degree in psychology from the 60s. No way, José! For a while I chickened out. A few days later I calmed down. I had also had time to establish that counselling was a legal necessity to progress. I resigned myself, and a counsellor rang me.

A few phone calls later, and I felt very small indeed for having harboured such hasty thoughts about counsellors. I mentally ate large slices of humble pie. When my husband and I went to London to meet my counsellor and see my records, my theories were further shot to pieces. Sparing her no blushes, she is quite simply one of the nicest, most approachable, practical and professional people I have ever met. No Indian skirts, no dingy room, not a joss-stick in sight. How naïve I had been.

The story of my adoption was broadly what I had been told, except for a few details that you wouldn't tell a child anyway. My faith in my adoptive parents and their integrity took a huge leap upwards. They had told me the truth, even though sometimes it must have hurt them. I was impressed. The complete truth told a heartbreaking story and my sympathy went out to my birth mother who had indeed struggled against all odds and 'failed'.

No amount of preparation however could have braced me for the tidal wave of emotion that overwhelmed me when I read through a copy of the letter my birth mother had written to the nursery the day after she had left me there. She really had loved me, it really had broken her heart. She wrote with the words I would have used, and suddenly it was me giving my daughter up. It tore me in half, and I sometimes still cry if I relive the moment that I had an insight into the pain she had gone through. I had to find her.

All 'the books' tell you not to look through the telephone directory. But how do you resist when virtually the whole country is sitting in the local library? Soon there was a burning reason why I absolutely had to go to the library I hadn't visited for at least 15 years. When I emerged with photocopies of the appropriate surname in all potential parts of the country, I felt very naughty because I knew this wasn't the official way to go about things, but I felt good just possessing pieces of paper which must surely contain my mother's current address. Because I also hoped for a short cut, I joined NOR-CAP, hoping that my mother had heard about them and put herself on their contact register. She hadn't. At the same time I applied to the General Register Office to see a copy of my original birth certificate. Their system is a ponderous dinosaur but it eventually came up with the goods. There was no new information for me and I knew there wouldn't be when I applied, I just wanted the certificate for completeness.

Instead a search of the phone lists in the area where my mother's family had lived looked promising. She had an unusual surname, and there were a couple of likely candidates who had the initials of my birth uncles. With the help, but not, I suspect, the blessing of my counsellor, my husband who had been volunteered to do the dirty deed cooked up a bit of a fib of an excuse to ring these people up, looking for an 'old family friend'. Lies, damned lies, and people searching for their birth families. But it seemed too obvious a lead not to follow up and I didn't relish the prospect of St Catherine's House. My husband was fortified with a few whiskies (he doesn't lie well otherwise) and went out. (Brave, eh?)

The very first phone call yielded a birth cousin who innocently provided my birth mother's current address and name (she had remarried years before) without batting an eyelid. I fought down an overwhelming urge to jump into the car and drive through the night to find her. How could our search have been so easy? I had agreed with my counsellor that the first contact should be made on my behalf by the Society, and we decided to do so by letter. I must have shed serious fractions of a stone in weight waiting for the Society to receive a reply.

Yet within two days the counsellor rang me to say that my birth mother had rung her and left a message on the answering machine, saying that she was indeed my mother and wanted to have contact. I had to have that message played back to me four times. The voice of my birth mother. I cried my eyes out. I had no idea that this acceptance could mean so much to me and another wall of emotion hit me. This whole sequence of events was turning into an emotional roller coaster with bigger highs and lows than I had ever experienced in my life. I had no idea until I started to poke about at it, just how much I had denied myself and covered up. Up until then I had thought I was a fairly normal sort of person with negligible problems and hang-ups and with perfectly average emotions. Now I was resolving problems and filling in gaps in a psychological jigsaw I didn't even know I had possessed. And here I was crying like a baby at the sound of my mother's voice. This was getting heavy!

It was arranged that I should write to my birth mother, and she would write back. That sounded fine until I sat down to do it. Where do you start? What on earth do you say? It took me two weeks to come up with something! By return of post, back shot total acceptance on 17 pages of handwritten foolscap. More tears, more howling. I don't usually cry so much! What was happening to me? Shares in Kleenex would have been an asset! I rang her up immediately and we talked for hours, in the middle of the morning. Shares in BT would have been nice, too!

Ten days later my husband, my daughter and myself were travelling to meet my mother at my brother's. I had hardly slept and before I left I spent hours glued to the loo. I couldn't find anything suitable to wear. I looked haggard. I cried at a moment's notice so I didn't dare wear make-up! By the time we arrived at the house I was a nervous wreck. She had heard the car and was waiting at the front door as I got out. We slowly converged on the garden gate. It was an awesome moment and it seemed to last for a very long time. We just looked at each other, then she held out her arms and we hugged. 'Oh yes, you're one of mine!' she said. Minutes later, I met my brother. 'Hello!' he said, 'haven't seen you for a while!' It was for all the world like I'd never left. I had come home.

That was over two years ago. I have three brothers, two sisters and three step-sisters. It is a very big clan, for an 'only child'! Meeting them all has been very easy; we share a sense of humour (weird though it may be!) we like similar things, and have similar views on the world. I find them very comfort-

able people to be with. I have a little brother I never anticipated. I have become particularly close to the sister immediately older than me; my family went to her wedding and she is
a godmother to my second daughter.

Above them all reigns the matriarchal figure of my mother,
who is a pretty wonderful person, in my biased opinion! She
had kept my memory alive, each year entering my birthday on
the calendar along with the rest of her children. She had
helped herself and her family over my loss by believing that
our separation was only temporary and that one day I would
come back. As she puts it, "In my mind, your place was always
laid at the table". How did I get so lucky? But the potential
family doesn't stop there! My birth father had five children
before me, and the two families knew each other well. Most
still live in the same area and would be easy to contact. When
I mention looking for my father's family, my brothers recoil in
distaste. "You're our little sister, not theirs! You're one of us,
not them." My sisters, contrarily enough, think it's a great
idea and have offered to stage an expedition to the home town
to help me find them. That pot continues to boil.

There are many curious links between my birth family and
my adoptive life. My first daughter is called Evelyn May and
one of my grandmothers was called Eva May. One of our dogs
is called Flossie, which was the family name for one of my
other grandmothers. My mother shares the same birthday as
an adored uncle I lost a few years ago, and my first daughter
was christened on the same day as I was. In the same week as
I saw the fateful discussion programme, my two elder brothers decided together that they would try to find me, and a sister, acting on her own, had written a letter to the authorities
asking if there was any way in which she could find me. My
other sister, unable to have children of her own, has adopted a
little girl and the family has had to come to terms with adoption from the other side of the fence. Just coincidence?

But it isn't all a bed of roses. My adoptive parents took the
news of my search very badly. I have worked extremely hard
to be fair, honest and open with them without wishing to rub
salt into any wounds they might have, but I am not prepared
to lie to them about an issue as important as this. In response
they have shut themselves off completely, acting as if none of
this had ever happened. Our already ailing and fragile relationship has been further eroded and great gaps of mistrust
and misunderstanding have opened up despite all my efforts.

Other members of my adoptive family, uncles, aunts etc, have been extremely supportive, if necessarily discreet in their encouragement. One of my birth brothers met one of my adoptive aunts and the conversation had to be interrupted after over an hour!

The saddest part for me however has been the distance that has developed between me and my husband. We met as only children and shared a very close relationship, not only as husband and wife, but as best friends. He seems to feel threatened by the arrival of so many siblings to whom I relate so easily and who I think he believes, quite incorrectly, to be replacing him in some areas of our friendship. To all my original family I view my birth family as an addition and extension, not a replacement. My husband sees me as having changed profoundly since finding my birth family. He says I am more confident, more motivated and more forgiving of other people. But then a tremendous amount has happened in the last couple of years, so maybe I am all of those things. A lot of it is to do with becoming a mother, becoming a daughter and then growing up. Most people manage to do it the other way round! Nonetheless, these changes have helped to form a different person to the one he married, and he is not altogether comfortable with that. He feels less needed, he feels my time and affections have been diluted. I don't feel I've changed all that much at all, except in that I feel more complete, somehow; I've scratched a nagging itch, I've filled an empty hole, I've satisfied a gnawing hunger. It had to be done but I didn't know that finding out a few facts about my past would change my present relationships so profoundly.

The most lasting sensation from all of this is, perhaps surprisingly, one of isolation. Taking a step backwards, I see that I was never really a wholehearted part of my adoptive family, welcoming and generous though they were. I never looked like them, reacted like them, thought like them, I was just very well trained to fit in. But now I can also see that I don't belong to my birth family either. Thirty years apart, our different upbringing, different experiences in different parts of the country can never be replaced or wiped out. I am unbelievably lucky that both sides love me and consider me their own, but in truth I belong to neither. I belong where I have built my own life, my present and my future; with my husband and my daughters. I am my own small island, one created by circumstance a long time ago before I was aware of it, and populated only by the present and the characters in it. I am not sad or bitter about this – you cannot be bitter about circumstance, and at least I now know where I stand in the world. That knowledge alone is worthwhile.

So on balance, has it all been worth it? I leave the last word to my birth mother. When my sister got married last year, every single sibling turned up from all parts of the country. My mother was to be seen in a quite uncharacteristic frenzy, rushing around muttering "My babies, my babies! I've got all my babies together at last!" It was, in truth, quite a 'clan-bake'. She finally winkled out all her children, sat us in a big group, and took some photos. One in particular came out very well. Later she sent us all a copy. I rang her up:

"Thank you for the photo, it's great. Are you pleased with it?"

"Pleased with it? Pleased with it? You silly girl! I've painted the walls with it!"

BIRTH PARENTS'
ACCOUNTS

The following six accounts are written by birth parents. They reflect the wide range of feelings which surround tracing and reunions for them.

Anna

This letter was written to an adoption counsellor by Anna after she had been contacted with the news that the son she had relinquished for adoption 27 years previously wanted to see her.

"Dear Sarah

Just a few lines to thank you for getting in touch with me about Simon.

I did not think I would ever hear from him again, let alone see him. As you said on the phone, in those days it was seen to be wrong to have a baby without a father, there was no money to help you and your own family did not want to know you.

Giving Simon up for adoption was the only way out at the time. At least he had a chance in life with a couple who would love and look after him as I couldn't.

But Simon was always in my thoughts and prayers. Now we have a chance to get together and I can put him in the picture over things that happened.

I just hope he likes me when we see each other this weekend. I am glad he is coming here to my home as he can meet my husband as well, all at once. That way he won't be nervous meeting him after he sees me. My husband, Roger, is glad that Simon is coming this weekend specially to see me. He knows that Simon has been on my mind for so long. I've always wondered where he is, how he is, and other things as well, but now we have a chance to meet again.

It's like having your first born baby all over again. I'm over the moon. Nervous, glad and very pleased indeed all at once. I'm really in a world of my own.

I can't explain how I feel, but so very glad that we can be together again, even if it is only for a weekend. At least I know he is alive and well.

Sarah, I hope even after this, we can still write to each other. As I've told you on the phone, there are lots more things I want to know. Some things that at the moment I can't say until I've seen Simon.

Whenever you put the next mother in contact with her adopted child after many years, I hope she will be as happy as I am right now.

I just hope and pray it will be alright over the weekend. I'll write to let you know how it went."

Sonya

The following account was written by a birth mother who describes clearly the changing emotions and feelings after the reunion with her daughter.

"In 1967 I went out to New Zealand aged 23 mainly to meet relatives I had only heard about. Sadly, due to a shipboard romance, I ended up pregnant and desperate. It was a real stigma in those days but I was lucky in that I had cousins in Dunedin who let me stay and were marvellous and caring. I worked for a while to earn my keep until I went into hospital and had a beautiful baby daughter. I called her Tracey. At the time there was no question of an adoption for me and I intended to return to the UK with her. However I hadn't bargained on my parents saying no. "What would the neighbours say?" Also they felt I was too young for such a burden and my mother worked full time. I left the hospital still refusing to sign adoption papers.

Eventually I returned to Auckland feeling empty and desolate. The adoption papers arrived several weeks after the birth and there was no alternative but to sign. It passed in a daze. I forget a lot of the details of that time – I just shut it out. I continued to write for almost a year for news of my baby and received a few letters. One enclosed photos from the adoptive parents and I was told to be grateful and make no further contact and get on with my life.

I remained in New Zealand for a few years and married in 1969. I told my new husband all about Tracey. We returned to England in 1971 and neither of my parents ever mentioned the birth or the adoption and nor did I – it was locked away in my mind. I thought of her at birthdays and wondered.

On 8 February 1988 an envelope marked O.H.M.S. with a Dunedin postmark arrived through the letterbox. I knew what it was after all those years, but I was unprepared for such an unleashing of feelings that overwhelmed me when I opened the letter. There were three – one from the Adult Adoption Information Officer, another from the adoptive mother and finally one from 'my daughter'. I cried solidly for three days and felt as if I were on I high.

It took me three days to answer the letters. Life was unbearable until the reply came – with photographs. I studied them over and could see a likeness to our daughter (aged 14) as a baby, but not to our son (aged 11) nor to me, although my husband said he could. About three months later when returning from shopping my husband said, "Your daughter has phoned." I couldn't believe it and she later rang back – to make sure I was real, she said! It was wonderful. For the next six months I floated on cloud nine but gradually came back down to earth, though I still hung on to every letter. I had also started writing regularly to her adoptive mother, who sounded very nice and extremely supportive and encouraged the contact between us.

Then came the news that she was coming to England to meet me. The time had come to tell our children. We sat them down and my husband explained the situation. My daughter immediately understood, as there was a reunion taking place on TV's *Neighbours*. My son said, "Are there any brothers anywhere?"! It really helped and made us laugh.

I had also told my mother six months after initial contact was made. She burst into tears but seemed pleased.

My daughter and my cousin arrived at Heathrow in July 1990. It was a nerve-wracking time. I felt sick with worry. Would she like me? Did she look like me? Would she regret coming? It was an emotional meeting. I kept sneaking looks at her as we went back to the car and I just couldn't take it in. She was tired and tearful and slept most of the way home. She was composed meeting my mother and our children until she went up to her room and saw flowers and a big welcome banner, and then it was tears all over again and she said it was something she had dreamed of all her life.

We got along quite well, though it was difficult and to be frank, she got along better with my husband than with me, which I resented. I took her to Scotland for one week to meet my father's family. He had died some years before, but I know that he would have been thrilled to meet her – more so than my mother, who has not told any of her family and friends and sees no point in it.

We talked quite a bit – it wasn't easy and I didn't remember too much especially about the father, as I knew very little and selfishly I hoped she didn't want to contact him. I found the whole thing quite stressful but still I was so pleased to have her in my home. We went to London – we both love shopping and had quite a bit in common, I think. She wasn't easy to talk to – she is reserved but friendly and she has obviously had a happy, loving, caring upbringing for which I am very grateful, but we found it difficult to share our feelings and the pressure on us both was enormous. The month passed quickly and it was an emotional goodbye at the airport. I hope she found the visit worthwhile – I did. Whether I would ever have tried to trace I cannot honestly say.

We continued to write until February 1991 when we all went to New Zealand to see my husband's family and of course my daughter and her family. The visit was not a success. I had expected too much. It was difficult for her with both 'Mother' and 'Mum' together and I don't think she knew how to react, although she is not demonstrative towards her mum. Her parents made us welcome but it was all very tense. We met her boyfriend, now husband, and he and I got along very well. The children fitted in well and we had one really relaxed evening at my daughter's and her boyfriend's home with her parents and my cousins, but put her and me on our own and we fizzled. She didn't seem to want to spend time alone with me and seemed preoccupied and moody. It was a friendly goodbye, no tears, and I think she was relieved when we had gone. It was to be many months before I heard from her and I fretted. When a stiff impersonal letter finally arrived I in turn took ages to reply – I didn't know how to or even if I wanted to.

On her birthday last year I rang her with some trepidation. She was getting married in October and had sent an invitation. The floodgates opened again – the feelings were all still there. I desperately wanted to be there to share in something in her life. For lots of reasons I couldn't go but rang them on their big day. It was very tearful indeed, but I think she knew how much I had wanted to be there and I felt she wanted me there just as much.

We are all still hoping to visit New Zealand this July. I am keeping my fingers crossed that things will go well. I shall try not to expect so much and I hope the tenseness and pressure won't be there this time. I hope she will want to keep me in her life. There is still so much I don't know about her. I would like to have a 'special' relationship with her. After all, I can never be her Mum – she has a Mum and Dad and I am Mum to our two children. Time will tell.

I hope that when my daughter and her husband have a family she will realize the feelings I had and how she might feel at having to give her child away. It was a bereavement and I didn't realize how much pain there was that I had shut away until she found me."

Ann

Although Ann was pleased to be contacted by her daughter, she had not expected to be contacted, nor had she yearned for it to happen.

"I gave my baby up for adoption during World War II. I never expected any further contact and news. The actual separation, after looking after my daughter for two months, was traumatic. But I didn't have much time to think about it, with a new job and very busy life-style.

Having effectively put the episode out of my mind for 40 years, it was a tremendous shock when my daughter traced me.

I was very nervous about meeting my daughter but I was supported well by friends and by The Children's Society. A friend came with me to the actual meeting, whilst my daughter brought her husband. At first I did not immediately think, 'this is my child'. However, as time went on, I started to feel closer to her.

I think that it has been quite a strain on my daughter as surprisingly she has herself adopted three children who are now in their teens. Her adoptive father died some years ago and her mother is now elderly, so her daughter has not been able to talk to them about it. I think she is also worried about telling her children that she has traced because she is afraid that it will encourage them to trace their birth families too.

I think that I would have been perfectly happy if I had not been traced – it was not something constantly on my mind like it is with some birth mothers. Even so, my daughter and I now correspond fortnightly and there are frequent phone calls and visits."

Cynthia

Cynthia married her son's father after the adoption and describes the added dilemmas this brought to her reunion.

"When I first got the letter from The Children's Society, I knew what people mean when they say the world stood still. Peter was 27 and I was not expecting to hear anything from him. I had thought about any possible contact when he was 18, but not now. I could not understand the letter and had to read it three times, and then felt absolute joy that he was alive and well. After that, the practicalities set in. I was happily married with a 20-year-old daughter. The rest of my family knew about Peter but would they want to be reminded of that unhappy time? How would it affect everyone else?

My own wishes were quite simple. Of course I wanted contact with him again. I wanted reassurance that he was coping with life, that my decision to have him adopted hadn't blighted him in any way. I was also very curious to know what he was like. I felt it wasn't 'fair' not to write to him. I thought it would be like another rejection, if he felt that his adoption had already been one rejection. I didn't understand why he wanted to have any contact with me and I didn't want to hurt him, so I agreed to write to him, giving details about my family and background. I also didn't tell him that I had later married his father and that our daughter was his sister. I thought at first that he might only want details about his background.

The first shock was when he sent photographs of himself, his wife and child. I knew logically that he was 27 years old, but I only had a photograph of him as a baby and I was still writing letters to an image of that baby. He was also the image of his father. I had not pictured him as a grown man able to make his own decisions. In my mind, I was still fighting battles for him and protecting his feelings, fighting off school bullies etc.

He was still writing and saying he would like to meet. I still hadn't told him who his father was, that I had knowingly given The Children's Society wrong information about the identity of his father and that we had actually married soon after the adoption. Nor had I told him that I hadn't told my daughter or family.

I still didn't know what he wanted from the meeting, although I knew I wanted to see him. But I wished he couldn't see me. His letters were always complimentary to me, but I knew I didn't deserve any of the nice things he wrote. I was overweight (OK I am fat), I smoke, I drink and I have never done anything in the least bit earth-shattering in my life. I thought he would be very disappointed, if not completely disillusioned, but I couldn't miss the opportunity of seeing him just once, even if it was the last time. Purely selfish reasons.

We met in a Steak House for dinner. We were both so nervous. There were so many questions to ask, but I didn't know what answers would upset him or what questions were taboo. His features were so familiar that in some ways it felt incestuous to be there. It felt like a first date. I couldn't eat anything and all I wanted to do was sit and stare at him. I had never believed in the power of genes, but he was so like his father in his manners, his thoughts, his ideas. Those two hours were some of the happiest in my life. I was so proud of him. I wanted to tell everyone he was my son, but I could take no credit for what he had turned out like. I felt like his mother. I felt the same about him as I felt for my daughter. If I could have, I would have kidnapped him and tried to catch up on the past 27 years.

After that meeting, I agonized over whether to tell him about his father. I could not make a decision as all I wanted was to see him again, but this would affect too many other people. I still wasn't sure what his feelings were or whether one meeting was all he wanted, and I couldn't write or see him again without telling him about his father. I still don't know what sort of mother he was expecting.

I wrote to The Children's Society and told them everything and they broke the news to Peter. He wasn't upset and wrote that he would like to meet us. I then had to tell my daughter. Everything went awry. At first she thought I was telling her that we were getting a divorce, then that we were retiring abroad, and then that I was giving her a sex lesson. When we finally got to the end, she was so overjoyed. She had always wanted an older brother, she didn't feel disgusted or ashamed of us. All she wanted to do was tell everyone. After two days, a reaction set in. She said she was angry with us. She felt 'displaced'. She couldn't explain it any better and went to stay with a friend. We still talked on the telephone and I took my frustrations out on the cooker and spring cleaning the house. After three days, she came back home and said all the anger had gone and she wanted to meet Peter and his family. She was back to normal.

We then arranged to have Sunday dinner together.

The Sunday dinner went off very well. My daughter is very lively and my husband provided distractions. Some British 'stiff upper lip' with dollops of Spanish emotion, general talk with everyone thinking and observing. My daughter said she sat looking at Peter for half an hour trying to think where she had seen his eyebrows before. Then she said to herself "he has my eyebrows". He looks and feels so familiar and yet I don't know much about him: likes and dislikes, prejudices, emotions, whether he had measles.

My husband thinks of Peter as our son but we are very economical with showing any emotions, as we are still not sure how he feels and don't want to frighten him. I would like to see a lot more of Peter and his family, but the practicalities of distance and earning a living get in the way. He also has his own parents and family and his wife's family, and I don't feel I can put too much pressure on him to meet. I still feel as if I have to be on my best behaviour in case he may decide he would never want to meet me again, whereas he is just perfect – but then doesn't every mother think like that?

I don't think anything can describe the emotions of the last five months. For every up, there was a down, and I found it impossible to keep everything in perspective and unbiased. All I wanted to do was to see Peter and get to know him. I would go to sleep thinking of him and wake up with my teeth clenched thinking of him. I think the contact was easier because he was older. Also the delays in meeting and writing help some of the emotions to dissipate. To pour out all of the feelings bottled up for the past 27 years would set anyone off running in the opposite direction."

Bev

The following account was written by Bev, a birth mother who describes movingly the pain both in giving her son up for adoption and in tracing him only to discover that he had died.

"Can a woman forget her own baby and not love the child she bore? Maybe for a time, but so many things trigger off the grief of parting and loss. For myself, sometimes I just sob when something triggers my memory. I press down feelings and grief because that is what I have learnt to do.

No one to talk to and some of the people I had told opened their mouths, although they promised they would not tell anyone. The neighbours must not know, the relations must not know; yes it's best to have the baby adopted because the new parents can give the baby so much more. But how does anyone know that?

I was just being left to get on with it – it's my fault anyway. I knew what I was doing so just put me away three months before the baby is due so no one is embarrassed by the bump. But I feel the baby move for six months, I wonder if it will be a boy or a girl. My breasts get larger and leak. I wonder if I should feed the child or will it make it harder to part after three months if I do? How can I possibly give my baby away? It doesn't seem right, but what else can I do? My mum is pregnant too and due three months before me and now I have spoilt the occasion for my parents. I love my boyfriend and would do anything to please him but to give my baby away, how could I? It's a part of me and him. But how can he feel the same for it because he is not feeling it move? He doesn't want to marry me because he doesn't really love me after all, only said he did to get his own way. But oh, the guilt and the shame. Perhaps I can run away? Where would I go? My Gran loves me but then all the relations would know and perhaps she wouldn't want the baby either.

I got taken to the mother and baby home in September 1960. At least everyone is in the same boat. One girl is only 12. Another girl's Mum and Dad came after a month to take her home and her boyfriend can marry her. "Stuff what the neighbours think," her Mum said. Another girl went to a party and got drunk and doesn't know who the baby belongs to. But I still see my boyfriend and he said he will stand by me but is not with me. He doesn't earn much money and I have to be practical and put the baby first. I feel trapped and scared. I go to church from the mother and baby home because it's run by the church.

The baby was due on 8 December 1960 but it started to arrive on the morning of 27 November 1960. What should I do? Because when you go into the labour ward you are on your own until the baby comes. No one to hold your hand and tell you what will happen. My baby was born and I was so thankful he was alright and I relaxed and cuddled him and marvelled at him and named him all by myself. They said the adopted parents would probably change the name, but to me he would always be Mark – Mark Andrew.

How can I give Mark up?! It's cruel. If I kept Mark, could I keep my boyfriend as well? – who do I love the most? How could I support my son? They say the adopters really want the baby and cannot have children themselves and they have nice homes and can look after them really well and are desperate for children. I can always have more children – but I can't have Mark again. He had to go to a children's home for a while because he wasn't feeding properly. It was only ten miles from my home and I had to hand over my baby to a stranger in the Matron's office and leave him forever.

My Mum baths my brother but I feel so empty. One day I couldn't stand it and I went to see Mark. He was in a room with other babies. I cuddle him and feel so useless but I have to push down all those feelings and do the 'right' thing.

Mark was adopted after two months and I signed the adoption papers.

My boyfriend and I got married in 1963 and in 1964 and 1966 we had two more sons. The pain faded but never went away. Our first son after marriage was born on 30 November 1964, four years and three days after Mark's birthday and we called him Andrew Mark. Our sons were never told about Mark and my husband did not want to talk about it, so I had to keep it buried.

I was told that the adoptive parents are advised to tell the children they are adopted when they are 18 years old and give them their full birth certificate with the birth mother's name on and details, so I was hopeful that Mark would get in contact with me when he was about 20 years old, as I could not contact him. Then in 1990 I watched a programme on television about birth mothers' experiences. I was at home by myself, as my husband was on the night shift. At the end of the programme they gave a helpline number and I phoned and was advised to write to NORCAP.

I was told that Mark might have been adopted through The Children's Society and 14 months later I wrote to them and, yes, Mark was adopted through them. What will I do if he does not want contact? But just to know that he is OK and to tell him that we married and that he has two real brothers. But supposing he is a drug addict or the adoption did not work out?

We are told that Mark has been dead for two years. It was like loosing him twice. My husband cried for our son. We cried together for the first time over him. Our other two sons do not know the secret we have kept all these years and now we are grieving for the son we have lost. My husband only saw him once and I only knew him till he was two months old. Why grieve? Because we are birth parents and the bond cannot be explained, only God knows.

We were told that Mark was full of fun and life, he had bags of energy, he was bright, he loved pets and had an adoptive sister and brother and died aged 19 years 7 months in a car accident. His Bible was given to his girlfriend. They were going to be engaged the following week. The church was packed for his funeral. Many people approached his parents and told them of Mark's kindness to them. He was a very lovable and much loved young man and I would have loved to have seen him just once. But because of my faith in Jesus Christ, I believe that I will meet him in heaven.

"Can a woman forget her own baby and not love the child she bore? Even if a mother should forget her child, I will never forget you."

Isaiah 49 v 15 (Good News Version)."

Michael

Michael traced his daughter but was very conscious that their relationship must develop at her pace.

"In August 1988 I read in a newspaper of a man who was frantic to trace his two daughters who had been adopted by his former wife and her new husband after her remarriage. The newspaper advised that it was not illegal to attempt to find his daughters aged 19 and 21 but that it would be very difficult. He was also advised to leave his details with the General Registrar's Office Adoption Section which was then based at Titchfield. I cut out this article and kept it until November 1989 when I wrote to the people at Titchfield to see if they could help me, as my girlfriend had placed our daughter for adoption in 1965. I had not agreed with her decision but was not asked for my opinion nor interviewed by anyone with any authority.

Also in late 1989 I saw an advertisement in my local paper about a group for anyone who had parted with a child for adoption. Eventually I found the courage to telephone them. I was worried that they would not want to talk with a father, that they might see me as the cause of the problem – but they were so helpful and understanding and sent me some leaflets including information about BAAF and NORCAP.

I contacted both organizations and sent my details to the adoption society. I also had to make a statutory declaration that I was the father of my girlfriend's daughter for the General Registrar's Office. Within a few weeks I had made sure that if my daughter ever decided to seek her birth parents, my details would be waiting for her wherever she might begin her search.

In August 1991 she made that move and contacted the adoption society. I had a birthday coming up in September – would I get a card? I wondered. I did much better than that – I received a letter, a card and two photographs. I just cried and when I went to bed I put the photo beside the bed; I kept waking up and saying to myself, is this true? Is this really a photo of my daughter, the daughter I have never seen?

It is very important to have this contact by letter via an intermediary. When you do get a letter don't write back by return, give it a few weeks, read it and digest it, talk to others about it. I did and after about three months my daughter asked to meet me. You must not push it, they will ask to meet when they are ready. She knew I was wanting to meet her as I had put that down on my details which I left with the adoption society, but I had not referred to it in any more correspondence as you could frighten them off. Once contact has been made, they will meet you.

I met my daughter in December 1991. She had her Dad with her as she was a bit apprehensive, which is understandable. We had a chat for more than an hour. I made it a three-way conversation and then asked about taking photographs, which my daughter agreed to. I also asked her Dad, the only Dad she has known for 26 years, if it was all right with him. I felt this was the point where he felt I was not going to steal his daughter. I also made sure I got him in some of the photographs. I felt this was very important as then when the photographs were shown around, people could see that reunions can work. I made it very clear that her Dad and Mum would be very welcome to come and see me at my house anytime.

My daughter then wrote and said she was pleased we had met. After five months, my daughter asked if she could come and see me and bring her Mum. This meeting also went very well. As she is the mother of four adopted children, she always felt that one day a birth parent would want to make contact and was ready for it and spoke quite openly about it.

I did not ask them any questions or details, I just let them tell me what they wanted me to know. I made it clear to my daughter's Mum that she could contact me at any time for a chat if she wished. She did write and thank me for the visit and said she was very pleased to meet me. It is still early days and I am going along with my daughter's wishes to keep in touch via a friend away from the main family, as they don't want to upset the other children who may want to start their search and who might not be as lucky as my daughter was.

I would advise all birth fathers to be persistent with your enquiries, don't give up and do go along to your local NORCAP group – that is where you will get help and support."

ADOPTIVE PARENTS' ACCOUNTS

In this chapter three adoptive parents share their experiences of reunions. Each has been affected in different ways.

Claire

This is an account of an adoptive parent's experience of her daughter, Deborah, tracing and finding her birth family. Deborah's mother, Claire, had died. (Deborah's account is on pages 38-39.)

"It is now well over a year since Deborah traced her birth family. This time has had its share of happiness and sorrow.

Ten days after she was 18, Deborah asked if I would mind if she traced her birth family – she was adopted by us as a baby, as was her brother two years earlier. I said I didn't mind and would help, but she had already been to see a counsellor. She showed me all the papers the counsellor had given to her.

Suddenly names on paper were 'real' people. This was a very strange feeling, as although I had thought a lot about her birth mother over the years, they are 'distant' thoughts because you can't have a picture in your mind. However, that evening we were both very excited. It had been her dream for years to do this, although I hadn't known.

The events of the next few days are still firmly in my mind. As Deborah's mother's parents had moved from the area, it was easier to contact her birth father to ask about Claire's whereabouts. The counsellor made this first contact one Saturday morning and David told her he thought Claire was dead. We had to wait all weekend until Monday before he confirmed it and the counsellor rang to ask me to tell Deborah.

It was then arranged that Deborah should speak to David and after this phone call, they agreed to meet. He took her to where she was born and showed her where he had lived before she was born. It was a very odd feeling when she went to meet him, but I knew from what the counsellor had told me that he was very, very happy to hear about her – he had even remembered her birth weight.

She has seen him quite often and although the first few months seemed to be 'up and down', her relationship with David has deepened into a great friendship and also with Sarah, his girlfriend. Neither David nor Claire had any more children, and Claire had died a year before Deborah started to trace her.

A few months ago, Deborah decided to try and find Claire's parents and our counsellor started the search by writing to Claire's husband – David had given the address to Deborah. They were so pleased, and I spoke to Jean, Claire's mother. This was so emotional for us all, and I think Deborah found it very hard. We arranged to meet – we went to see them and visited Claire's house and also went to her grave.

The days after this visit were the hardest for all of us because of the very great sadness we all felt about Claire. Deborah learned so much more about her, but it was such a sad story. Mike, Claire's husband, is such a lovely person and feels they have all got 'a bit of Claire' back.

We have seen them twice since that first visit and keep in touch.

How do I feel about it all?

At the very beginning it was exciting and then frightening – they may not have wanted to know etc. Then it was sad and I cried a lot for Claire, for Deborah who was so upset, and very much for Jean and John who had lost their only child in tragic circumstances. Also Claire had never forgotten and had kept a photograph we sent to her via the Society. She always hoped to see her again.

Having said that, David is delighted, Deborah gets on very well with him and at the time of writing she is staying with them. Jean, John and Mike are also very happy she found them. We haven't met David – his choice, not ours – but I've spoken to him occasionally. I'm more than happy to share, as long as it works out well for Deborah and we have been much closer to each other since it all happened. I'm very glad she did it, and although I know she always 'wanted to know', it must have taken a lot of courage.

Our son does not want to know anything, and has no desire to trace anyone. I hope his mother is happy because having heard how Claire had suffered, I even at one point felt a bit guilty that I had been so happy when other people were devastated at letting their baby go.

A very important part of all this has been our counsellor. I would say always talk to your counsellor. It was so helpful for us to have someone to calm everyone down and to chat to Deborah. It wouldn't have been half so easy without her."

Sandra

Sandra did not know that her daughter wanted to trace her birth family, although she had always been very open with her and said she and her husband would support her. Her letter to her daughter's counsellor describes clearly the feelings that adoptive parents can have when this happens.

"Now that the 'dust has settled' since Laura found her mother and I can think rationally again, I would like to make a few comments from the 'social' mother's point of view.

I know from discussions with Laura that she had considered the implications of her arrival in her 'new' family and that she had been carefully counselled by you. I must confess to feeling some sadness that as her adoptive family, we were not involved in any discussion prior to the reunion with her mother. In common with most young people, Laura was quite unable to estimate the impact her 'good news' would have on us. She has since told me that you had asked her what our reactions were likely to be and that she told you we'd be fine. Unfortunately, although we have never attempted to conceal the truth from her and we understand her natural wish to find her roots, it is impossible to predict how one is going to react when the moment of discovery arrives. Perhaps this applies especially to the mother, whose status is suddenly changed – certainly my husband was more logical than I was!

Part of the problem was that Laura gave me her news on the phone rather than face to face. She was so obviously joyful and excited, having just had a long conversation with her mother, who "sounded lovely" and wanted her to come and stay immediately. Everything happened with such speed and at a distance that I felt stunned. However well you think you have prepared yourself, it is a tremendous shock to hear your child call someone else 'mum' after being so deeply involved with her for 19 years. It is impossible to remain detached.

As you will no doubt have discovered from talking to her, Laura is very direct, determined and anxious not to waste time, hence the speed with which she went to meet her new family. I am extremely thankful that I was able to see her soon afterwards and discuss my fears frankly, otherwise there would have been considerable misunderstanding on both sides. She was both surprised and disappointed at my initial response to her news – she thought I was being selfish when I should have been happy for her. While this is no doubt true, Laura has not experienced trying to combat the possessive nature of parental love which cannot be entirely selfless. Having to 'hand her back' left me with a sense of bereavement and it was a nerve-wracking experience, as I expected her to be changed.

The obvious attraction of having a young and lively mother instead of a 'jaded nag' I can well appreciate! But the thought of her possibly making unfavourable comparisons between the two families made me feel very defensive, particularly with regard to her two younger brothers. The whole family, and Laura in particular, has suffered considerable misery as the result of the behaviour of our eldest son, who is also adopted but has no wish to find his mother. While I believe that the experience has made Laura a stronger person, I felt that the new family might provide her with 'a bolt hole' when she is under pressure. I was greatly reassured (and amused) by her assessment of me as 'very insecure', that she has no intention of leaving home and that she feels quite able to cope with two families.

My main concern now is for Laura's future and her gradual integration into her 'new' family – she is meeting her grandparents this weekend when she returns for her second visit to Manchester. It is certain that they will want to see her regularly and while we have no intention of discouraging her from visiting, I fear that her loyalties may be divided, leading her to feel guilty. She already feels a sense of responsibility towards her mother and young brother.

Although I partly agree with Laura that 'the child must come first', I feel it is equally important to remember that other people are involved as well as her. She has approached her mother's family with great sensitivity, but since she knows us so well she thought it was unnecessary in her dealings with us. For this reason I have left her to tell her brothers at home when she feels the time is right, and when she can see their reaction for herself.

Although I am successfully coming to terms with the idea that we are not Laura's only family, I feel some disquiet that the adoptive family ceases to have any 'rights' once the child is

18. This is no doubt inevitable since he/she is an adult and can dictate the terms and the pace. As Laura reminded me, she could have gone behind our backs, which while it would have been out of character, clearly insinuated 'it's none of your business'! However, I feel strongly that the adoptive family should have the right to expect some loyalty from the child. Perhaps like Laura they underestimate the depth of love and commitment which the adoptive parents give, in the belief that they are 'different' from other children. Having under-valued themselves, they do not expect the adoptive family to mind 'losing' them. Certainly Laura thought we were impervi-ous to hurt.

Contrary to her expectation, the possibility of her return to her mother was not discussed when we adopted her because original birth certificates were not available then. I under-stand that adopted children need to find their birth parents in order to feel 'completeness'. But I am sure that I am not the only adoptive mother who finds it difficult to overcome the sense of failure which results from her child's need to seek an alternative."

Michelle

Michelle describes her shock and sadness at discovering that two of her adopted children had begun tracing their birth families but had kept this secret from her.

"My husband and I adopted three babies. Richard is the eldest and is now 39, Jeremy is 37 and Jane, who lives in Los Angeles, is now 34 years old. Sadly in 1988 my husband died of cancer.

Jane has a baby daughter and I have recently been to see them in Los Angeles. We had a wonderful holiday and, being very close, Jane and I were able to speak frankly to each other about all sorts of things.

Two days before I was due to come home, when Jane was in the bedroom with the baby and I sat in the sitting room, I opened a magazine to read. Out fell a letter. I recognized the writing as being that of my son, Jeremy. Jane had already read a few sentences from the letter a few days previously, and I thought I would just finish reading it. Much to my dismay and sadness I read that Jeremy was in the process of searching for his birth mother. He had written and told Jane how far he had got, and he asked her how she was coping with her situation.

I immediately went to find Jane and told her that I had read her letter and asked what it all meant. Finding out so suddenly and unexpectedly was an enormous shock to my system and we sat on the bed together and we cried and we kissed and we hugged and the whole story came out.

My husband became ill in 1987 just before Jane was due to be married and he was too ill to go to the wedding. So Jane and her husband came over in January 1988 and we gave her her adoption papers for the first time, with her own mother's name and address. She had to have that in order to get a visa to stay in the United States. Because she was going to be here for several months, she decided to follow up the information she was given on those papers. She found that she had to have some counselling before taking her search any further. After a very short while she found that her birth mother was living in

Dorset and they met up.

What an enormous help it had been to her birth mother to hear the full story of Jane's life. Listening to Jane telling me this, I felt most of all a tremendous sense of loss, without quite knowing why.

Jane explained to me why she had not told me before – that at the time my husband had been so ill and she quite rightly realized that it would be too much for me to bear. She was afraid of what the consequences might be. Jane also told me that Jeremy and Richard had discussed tracing and that Richard had no interest in finding his birth mother. Jeremy, however, was more curious but decided to let Jane trace her birth mother first.

I spent the entire flight home thinking about it all. I felt sadness that I hadn't been told right from the beginning. It was almost as though it had been a *fait accompli* and I had been left out of a very, very important family decision. Had I known, if my husband had not been ill, I'm sure both of us would have been only too happy to help them in their searches.

I did feel strongly that Jane had done the right thing and that it was very important for her to put the last piece in the jigsaw puzzle. I had told her so before I left. And I fully understood her position – if I had been her, I would have probably done it many years before. But I still feel sad that I didn't know about it all at the beginning.

Soon after I arrived home, I decided that it was important for me to speak to Jeremy. He found it quite difficult to talk but he showed me papers I hadn't seen before relating to his adoption. Of course it brought back all the memories of the adoption years ago.

I do think speaking to Jeremy was an enormous help for both of us. We aired a lot of thoughts that we hadn't spoken about before. It is obviously extremely important for Jeremy to trace his mother. So far he has not had any success. Seeing his father's name on the papers upset him greatly. I think it was because he realized for the first time that he had a different surname. I have told him all that I know about his birth mother, which is not much, but he was grateful for that and found it a help.

So we still have a long way to go. He may in fact never find her but he does feel even if that happens he has at least tried. And that will satisfy his own mind a little. Jane understands exactly how he feels.

I have also spoken to Richard and sent him his adoption papers but he is quite happy and seems to accept the identity that he has found for himself. At the moment he has no desire to search for his birth mother. This may of course change in the future and I shall also have to be ready to help him.

As for myself, I do find that each day it gets a little easier. I also think that I have had a fear of losing Jane's love. I was afraid that because she has now found her birth mother she would no longer look on me as her mother, but that hasn't been so. She did write me a wonderful letter when I reached home explaining that all the years she had had with me were of importance and had gone into building her own character and that she felt that only a very small percentage of her life was due to her genes.

I was also afraid that we would be driven apart. In fact it has brought us very much closer together – Jane put this in her letter as well. That is a rather wonderful thing, considering that we have both been through a very traumatic time together.

One poem that has meant a great deal to me and has helped me is by Hugh Evan Hopkins. Perhaps it might be of help to someone else:

The Mystery of Suffering (last verse)

I will accept the breaking of sorrow which God tomorrow will to his son explain. Then did the turmoil deep within him cease. Not vain the word not vain, for in acceptance lieth peace."

THE ADOPTION CIRCLE

This chapter offers three perspectives on each of two reunions.

Kate, Mary and Susan

This account has been written by Kate who traced her birth mother in 1989.

"Ever since I can remember, I always wanted to trace my birth mother. My adoptive mother knew this and was willing to help me when I was 18. The notes that she had on my birth mother were always available for me to read and it was never a taboo subject.

In the early years of being a teenager, I was very eager to find my birth mother – mainly thinking that she would let me do this, that and the other, whereas my adoptive mother would not.

During many an argument with my adoptive mother, I came close to saying "I wish someone else had adopted me". I never did say it, as I knew it would hurt my adoptive mother too much and I always felt guilty for thinking it. At times like this, I would think to myself what it could have been like if someone else had adopted me. These thoughts always began with me being better off, spoilt with loads of money and parents that let me go out until all hours. I would then turn my thoughts to the other side of the coin – what if an 'unloving' couple had adopted me? This made me realize that I was lucky to have the family that I had.

Also during my early teens, I wondered if my birth mother had considered having me aborted. I *never* hated my birth mother, instead I felt grateful. If she had never made a mistake, I would not exist...

At about the age of 15, I wrote an essay for English at school. The basic gist of it was that my birth mother had come looking for me and was sitting in the car outside my house. She saw me go out in the evening and she didn't approach me. She just watched me and thought my adoptive parents had done a good job of bringing me up. I received a very poor mark for the essay and my teacher's comment was: "This is over imaginative and would never happen. Don't write stories like this again." This was really distressing as I longed to meet my birth mother.

As I got older, I became less 'obsessed' with meeting my

birth mother, but knew that when I was 18 I would try and find her. At 18, I went for counselling at The Children's Society. My adoptive mother knew everything that happened and was 'with me' the whole time and encouraged my search.

We quickly discovered my birth grandparents' phone number by searching the electoral roll and my adoptive mother phoned them. They were amazed at the phone call and arranged to meet us the following week. They wanted to meet me before telling their daughter. However, they could not keep the secret and they told her about me before they met me. I had a long phone call with my birth mother when we asked about eye and hair colour and other things to do with appearance.

I met my birth grandparents on the Wednesday at my home address with my adoptive mother. I found them very inquisitive and affectionate and I liked them very much.

On the following Sunday I visited my birth mother and her family at her home with my adoptive family. I was very apprehensive about the meeting. Part of me wanted to know everything and go 'steaming in' with hundreds of questions and the other part of me could hardly climb out of the car. My birth mother opened the front door and we had the same colour dresses on – was this coincidental or was there an underlying reason to it?

After a 'polite' lunch, my adoptive family went for a walk and my birth mother's family 'disappeared'. This left my birth mother and me to talk. I don't remember what we talked about but there were lots of questions asked and answers given. I was amazed at how much we had in common, not necessarily in looks, but more allergies, attitudes to life and the things that people don't believe to be genetic. After this first contact we agreed to meet again in the future and keep in contact.

I returned home with my adoptive family, feeling ecstatic and relieved. My birth mother was a 'normal' human being and I liked her. I did not feel that she was my mother but more the person that had brought me into the world and gave me a chance in life by having me adopted.

When we got home I went to the pub to celebrate and tell my friends. When I returned home, my adoptive mother was very quiet and looked worried. I sensed her reason for this and reassured her that she would always be my mother and I would not be going to live with my birth mother. Although she knew this, she needed me to tell her in my own words. I think it was also because the day had been fairly stressful and she was worried for me as much as for herself.

Since meeting my birth mother and grandparents, I have kept in contact with them. The number of times I see them has been reduced partly due to circumstances and also the fact that I do not 'need' my birth mother. By this I mean that we each know where the other is and both our curiosities have been satisfied and the questions answered. I have contact with my birth mother and grandparents either by phone or letter once a month and I see them about three times a year.

When people ask me what it was like the first time I met my birth mother, I find it very difficult to answer. The closest way I have found to describe it is that it's like meeting a relative for the first time at a funeral. Apprehensive at the thought of it and relieved once there, but still withdrawn and unsure.

For about the first year after finding my birth mother, it did produce a little tension between my adoptive mother and myself, but I think this was due to a number of reasons and not just the reunion. If I went to visit my birth mother I always had a sense of guilt and pity for my adoptive mother left at home with her daughter away. This made me feel that I had to reassure her on my return.

I am very close to my adoptive mother and I'm extremely grateful that she was so helpful and willing about me finding my birth mother. Until the time we first met my birth mother, she knew that I was her daughter and nobody else's. After a little reminding and reassuring she could feel this again.

I made a point, and still do, not to call my birth mother 'Mum' or anything else along these lines. My Mum will always be my adoptive mother and my birth mother, the one who brought me into the world. When my birth mother sends me a card, she signs it from "Mum number 2". I am happy with this as she realizes that she will never be my Mum and accepts this fact.

This story is not all roses though. Recently I tried to find my birth father. My mother obtained his phone number and rang him. He claimed not to be my birth father and did not want to know anything or give any information away. I was very upset at this as I was hoping for a double happy ending. However, I realize that this is not possible and I must live with the knowledge that I will never know my birth father."

The following account is written by Kate's mother, Mary.

"Eighteen and a half years ago, we went to collect my baby daughter. My son Robert was two years old and was very excited to be collecting a 'special' sister who would be adopted just like him. After the usual formalities we set off with two very smiling children in the back of the car. During the following five months, we were visited by an adoption officer to check us over and make sure that Kate had settled with us and was happy. In fact, if she cried once in a fortnight I would wonder whatever was the matter with her.

The date for the Court Order was fixed for November and up until that day we would feel a little apprehensive in case her birth mother changed her mind. However, all went well and Kate was legally made our daughter.

With both my children I used to tell them the special story of how they came to live with us from a few months old. At bedtime, once they were tucked up in their cots, I used to bend over them as not only did they get used to hearing this story long before they could even understand it, but it also helped me to feel relaxed about telling them.

Unfortunately, when the children were seven and five, my husband and I were divorced. Luckily, they did not seem affected by this. In fact, we all helped each other and they were both very stable and happy. If at any time during their childhood they wanted to know anything about adoption or their birth parents, I always told them. As they became teenagers, I showed them all the information that I had which was a brief description of their birth families.

During their childhood, the law was changed, enabling adoptive children to trace their birth parents. At first, I was a little worried and then decided that of course, if they wanted to find their roots, it was up to me to help them and it would be another venture we would try as a family. My son made vague noises about tracing his birth father, but so far nothing has happened.

When Robert and Kate were 12 and ten years old, I re-married and with everyone in happy agreement, Jim adopted them as his own children. We all decided it would be rather nice to have another baby but until I was 40 this did not happen. Obviously, it was quite a surprise when Jill came into the world, but Robert and Kate were so thrilled with their baby sister and have been very good with her ever since. I must say here that having two children that were born in my heart and one under it showed me that there was no difference in the way that I felt for them – I loved them equally.

On Kate's 18th birthday we had a lunchtime party with family and friends. We had discussed searching for her birth family and after a few months she was put in touch with a counsellor with the Society, who saw her on two occasions and rang us at home. She was extremely helpful and gave Kate confidence and support. She was given her birth parents' address at the time she was born, but unfortunately was told by directory enquiries that they no longer resided there. It was a bitter blow as that meant Kate would have to join other organizations to help her and it was obviously going to take a long time. But luck was round the corner in the shape of my sister-in-law who worked in the town where Kate was born. After work one day, she went through the electoral roll and gave us four names and addresses of her birth family's neighbours at that time who were still living there.

With permission from Kate's counsellor, I rang their numbers, shaking from head to foot. The first two I contacted drew a blank, but the third was so helpful and not only gave me the address of Kate's birth mother's parents but also the telephone number. As it was Christmas time, we decided to be patient and wait until the celebrations were over, as we did not want to upset them.

One afternoon in January, I decided the time had come. Kate knew about it and found it hard to concentrate at college that day. I rang the number and it was answered by Kate's grandfather. I asked to speak to his wife as I felt that perhaps a woman might take it better. After all it was going to be a tremendous shock and I did not want him to be angry. I need not have worried. Having explained who I was, Rachel, although shocked, was as I imagined – a delightful person. After all, she was Kate's grandmother and as Kate is lovely, I felt sure that her birth family would be too. I did not ask about Kate's birth mother other than was she alright. In fact, I kept the phone call brief and suggested I rang again that evening giving them time to talk it over and get used to the idea.

The excitement in our house was enormous. We all felt relief that so far it had all gone well. The second telephone call confirmed this and I spoke to both grandparents who were so friendly and easy to talk to. Kate is only five feet two inches tall and I had often remarked that she probably took after her birth grandmother – this was agreed over the phone. We asked them to come to us for the day the following week, which they agreed. Kate's birth mother could not come due to a meeting at work, but we talked on the phone and planned to visit them the following Sunday. She said she had always hoped that Kate would find her. It was still a great shock to her. After all, by that time we had had six months to prepare ourselves and get used to the idea that contact could be made.

The grandparents' visit went well. We had a photo album out to show them a brief glimpse of Kate's life, and as we talked they could see family likeness. The following Sunday, we went as a family to visit Kate's birth family. Her mother had remarried and Kate found that she had a half-sister of 15 years old (called Tricia). Tricia had always known that she had an older sister and was looking forward to meeting her. On our arrival it was all too much for her. I think she felt threatened and disappeared upstairs for a while. Kate decided to put her mind at rest and promised her that she had no intention of taking her mother away but that it was curiosity that had made her want to find her roots. She pointed out that her mother was downstairs and that Tricia's mother had just brought her into the world. From then on they were friends. They certainly looked like sisters.

My one secret fear was that as Kate's birth mother was ten years younger than me, she would be a raving beauty. Obviously she was younger, but we were not unalike. The adoption society had made a good match.

My husband, Jill and I decided to have a walk after lunch leaving Kate with her birth family to catch up on many unanswered questions. It was not an easy day as I felt her birth mother was a little upset but she kept saying how glad she was that it had happened.

That evening Kate had gone to tell her boyfriend all about the day, my husband was out and Jill was in bed. Suddenly I felt drained and empty. For weeks I had been going along with Kate, excited for her and suddenly it was over and I felt very alone. I would have liked to put the brakes on then and not let it go any further but that would have been selfish as after all we had shown the birth family a lovely daughter and grand-daughter.

I have always discussed everything with my children and explained to Kate how I felt. I said that part of me was scared of losing her. She hastily assured me that that would never happen. She thanked me for making it all possible and said that she now felt 'complete'.

Since than she has visited her birth family once with her boyfriend and has met her aunt. However much environment plays a part in our upbringing, the hereditary factor is very strong and they have a lot in common. I feel close to Kate's new family and hope that we will continue to keep in touch as after all, we are all part of Kate's life."

This account was written by Susan, Kate's birth mother

Saturday 7th January started as a normal day for me. I went on duty in the morning as planned, but during my duty I had a message from my father to please telephone him. On finishing work, the phone call was made and he asked me to call and see them on my own please. I went straight to their house wondering what on earth was wrong.

My mother said they had something to talk to me about but did not quite know where to start. She started by telling me of a telephone call that they had received on Wednesday last, from a lady who she did not know, who went on to talk of an event 18 years ago. At this point I realized what was being said, and asked if it was Christine, the baby I had had adopted. Tears were now flowing, as yes, it was about her, but she was now called Kate and had been trying to find me along with the help of her mother Mary. At this point, I could not believe it. This was something I had dreamed of happening, as I had never forgotten her, but had always believed would never happen.

My parents were as shocked as I, and felt they had to tell me on my own as they did not know if my husband or children knew of this past event. But, yes, they did know. Before going back home, I telephoned the number that my parents had and spoke to Kate's father, Jim. Everyone else was out at that time. He sounded pleased that I had rung and would pass my message on when Mary returned. Kate was at work and not returning home until much later that evening.

There was so much I wanted to ask, but did not know where to start. It was still really too much to believe, but my parents had already arranged to go and meet Mary the following Wednesday, due to my work I would not be able to go, but felt that I wanted to meet her as soon as possible. At first they thought they would go and meet Mary before they told me anything, but my father could not keep it to himself any longer. I could not understand how they could have planned the meeting without telling me, but as time went on I realized they were doing it for my own good, so as not to build up my hopes, in case it did not work out. Maybe everyone would not get on, maybe Kate would be bitter towards our family, maybe we would all be very different.

I went home on a high with very mixed feelings, I kept asking myself, why? what does she want? what if she doesn't like me? or maybe I won't like her. I telephoned my husband (who was not Kate's father) as he was at work, and tried to tell him what had happened. Then I had to tell my children. I did not know what to say, so I told them straight that 'the baby I had had adopted who was now 18 years old had found me'. My son of 12 did not really understand, but my 15-year-old daughter wanted to know the full story. In between my tears I tried to explain to her, along with the help of my father.

On my husband's return from work, we talked and talked about Kate. I had her telephone number and decided to telephone again, in the hope of talking to her mother. When I first telephoned, I had not left my phone number or address, but I now felt that I did not object to them knowing where I lived. Her mother was at home and put my mind at rest over a lot of things. Kate had always been told that she was adopted and thought of her 'birth mother' on her birthday, just the same as I always thought of her on that day. She had backed Kate and helped in trying to find me. The phone call ended with me asking that Kate be given my phone number, and for her to ring me if she wished.

I then sat by the phone for the rest of the evening. At about 9.30 p.m. it rang, and yes, it was Kate. She was babysitting, so I rang her straight back. What do you say to someone after all these years? How do you explain events to them? What if I give the wrong answers to the questions she wants to ask? All these thoughts had been going through my head during the evening. But the telephone conversation was not like that. In among the tears from both of us we talked and talked. How tall are you? What colour is your hair? Your eyes? What do you do? We both tried to fill in the missing years. The call lasted well over an hour, but what did that matter? It ended with us agreeing that we wanted to meet, and as soon as possible.

It was arranged that Kate and family would come to my house the following Sunday.

During that following week I was very mixed up, half of me could not believe it, half of me kept asking, why me? I was scared of meeting her, but looking forward to it. I hated her, I loved her. What would my family think? How would my daughter, Tricia, react to meeting her? Would it upset my life as it was now? What did she want? Would I like her and her family? Would she like me or be disappointed when she met me? All these thoughts went round and round.

Mary had also given me the telephone number of a Children's Society counsellor. On Tuesday I rang her, as I felt I had to talk to someone who was not involved. She put my mind at rest, and explained how she had met Kate and how she was prepared for finding me, but what a shock it must have been for me, and that many people never try to find their birth parents and if they do how it does not always work out. Kate was prepared for all this, but if I needed to talk then I could phone or meet the counsellor if it would help, and how she hoped it would work out OK.

Wednesday arrived, and all day I kept thinking of how my parents were getting on. When the meeting was first arranged, they thought Kate would be at college and that they would only be meeting her mother, but Kate was to meet them as well. I kept on ringing my parents to see if they were home yet, but no answer came. They came straight to see me anyway on their return, armed with photographs for me to see. I kept on looking at the photos and wishing that tomorrow was Sunday.

Sunday arrived at long last, and I was on tenterhooks along with the rest of my family. What would I do when we met? At last they arrived and I put my arms around Kate, something I felt I would never be able to do again after she went to her adoptive parents all those years ago. Tricia found it all a bit too much coming face to face with a 'sister' she had never met before and went to her room. After a while Kate and I went to Tricia's room to talk to her. Tricia felt threatened, and that Kate would come between us. But Kate talked to her and put her mind at rest. All she wanted was to be friends and find out about her other family. She did not want to move in and take over. I was her birth mother, but her other mother was downstairs. Tricia was reassured by this and came down to join in looking at photographs of Kate from six weeks old to now, and Kate was shown plenty of photos of her other family. The day went very well with us all getting on well together. Kate and Tricia are so alike, not only in looks but in the things that they like to do.

I wonder now why I was so scared when first told, as things could not have worked out better. Our families were so alike, and what a wonderful job they had done of bringing Kate up, how lucky we all were that thinks worked out as they did. The day ended with an invitation for us to visit their home, and the hopes of a long and happy friendship to follow.

I have since met Kate again here, along with her boyfriend, and visited her home, where I, along with Tricia, feel a part of her family. Kate has also been to stay for two days and spent the time with Tricia. How great it is to see the two of them together. They get on so well together and I am so happy that we have found each other again, and hope for a long and happy friendship between both families."

Yvette, Monica and Shirley

The following three accounts have been written by Yvette, who was adopted, her adoptive mother Monica and her birth mother Shirley.

From an adoptive mother's perspective:

I always knew this day would come but my thoughts were "please God not this soon". Panic set in as my 'baby' (so grown up all of a sudden) sat on my bed and asked – "Mum, when will I be old enough?" and I knew straight away what she meant – to trace her birth mother, the subject having been raised many times over the years. No other Christmas present would do this year, I knew that. She was obviously not too young now. We would see this through together. She needed more than fairy tales about her past now.

It took all my courage to make that first call to The Children's Society. After all these years help was still at hand. The look on Yvette's face when I told her that night said it all – I had done the right thing, it was obvious. Relief that my part was over, and the responsibility now someone else's, was short lived. I was to be involved much more than I expected over the following year. After a very emotional Christmas and New Year, with my suddenly perfectly behaved daughter, the first meeting with the counsellor from The Children's Society was arranged. I was going to be the perfect mother and do the right thing without being selfish – but this wasn't easy. As those close to me will confirm, many tears flowed over the next few months and there were many sleepless nights. It was all happening far too quickly for me – ending in the day that Yvette and I spent together searching the Library records. More tears, more hugs when eventually what she had been wanting all these years was there in black and white – her birth mother's name, Shirley. She was so happy – how could I possibly let her know my fear that I was losing her?

With information on Shirley's reactions gradually filtering through to me from the counsellor the next few weeks brought sheer panic. I must say I went though hell, but at least

Yvette's dream was not to be shattered – that being the one fear her father had had.

I needed all the help offered when the day came for Shirley, Yvette and I to meet. For the first time in her life I saw Yvette nervous. The mixture of excitement in Yvette and apprehension in me made an atmosphere even the friend who came with me said you could cut with a knife. It was all tearing me apart. The exchange of letters had helped but nothing could prepare me for the way I felt.

It was now five o'clock and time to break it all up (much sooner would have suited me). What now? Do I shake hands or what? A quick hug came easily. Now completely mentally and physically drained, my friend and I walked off down the road leaving Shirley and Yvette making up for lost time. Crying once again – I was lost for words – what had I started? Am I losing my baby?! I was jealous of the hugs and kisses Shirley was getting but I needn't have been, I had plenty too when Yvette eventually came running up the road to join us. I shall always be grateful to both of them for being so sensitive to my feelings that day. Neither of them during their obvious excitement forgot how I was feeling.

Yvette meeting new members of the family is fitting in nicely with the normality of everyday life. I have seen part of Yvette never seen before – which confirms that my first instincts were right to allow and even encourage her to trace Shirley. An obvious void has been filled. I have benefited from the experience myself, with lots of affection coming my way as well.

My daughter is a young woman now and, even though I say it myself, one I am very proud of and hope Shirley will be as well. Having met and got to know Shirley a little, I suppose there is a lot of her in Yvette, but I hope we have contributed plenty over the years."

From Yvette

"My earliest memories of the adoption were when I was at primary school when I used to tell everyone. I always thought of myself as different but special because I had four parents.

As I grew older, I realized the need to find my birth mother to help me understand who I was and where I came from.

There has never been a time when I have held a grudge against my birth mother because I have always understood the reasons for her actions. However, there have been times when I used to think that she should have thought more of herself and not put me up for adoption.

The first time the subject of contacting Shirley, my birth mother, was raised was when I was 13. My adoptive mother did not see this as a good idea because I was so young and inexperienced and I now understand her decision, because the last six or seven months have been so traumatic for all involved.

Between that time and the end of last year the subject was raised many times, and it wasn't until Christmas 1991 that my adoptive mother, Monica, made a very painstaking decision and decided that I was mature enough, both mentally and emotionally, to go through with the procedure.

The big shock came for me at Christmas when Mum handed me an envelope. I had no idea what would be inside but I did have my suspicions. When I opened the envelope and read the card inside, my eyes welled up with such emotion, happiness and thanks for what Mum had done, when she knew it would put both families involved, especially herself, through so much pain and trauma.

It was not long before the first meeting with the counsellor from The Children's Society was arranged. This was necessary so that she could assess whether or not she thought I was able to cope with what laid ahead. Her own thoughts were that I was ready and able to continue what had been started but due to my age she also thought it necessary to confer with her colleagues to gain their opinions.

It was such a relief when I found out that they shared the same opinion as my counsellor. The next stage involved her sending a letter to Shirley's mother in Africa to obtain her present address. She also asked Mum and myself to get involved in the search and we were the ones who found the last piece of the jigsaw, so to speak. All that remained now was for my counsellor to make contact with Shirley to see if she was ready and willing to meet me. At this stage of the process, both Monica and I were asked to write a letter to Shirley, which would be passed on through my counsellor at their first meeting.

It was only when my counsellor told us that Shirley was willing to meet me that the reality of what was happening started to hit me.

Everything happened so fast that it wasn't long before the final day came and I was about to meet the person who had given birth to me.

Everyone was very on edge that Friday afternoon and to make things worse, we turned up an hour early. While we were waiting in The Children's Society offices the atmosphere was ever so tense. It was the first time I could remember in my entire life being nervous – or maybe scared is a better word to use. At one point during the waiting I asked to back out of the decision. Even now I don't know whether I was serious about that question or not. All I know is I am happy that no one would let me. My greatest fear of what was about to happen was that Shirley would not like me or be disappointed in me. I was relieved to find out that she wasn't disappointed and that she herself had exactly the same fears.

What happened that day was one of the most painful but happiest moments of my life. Not only do I have two mothers but I also have an extra brother and sister and I'm really glad that they have accepted me into their family and that we get on so well."

From a birth mother's perspective

"10 April 1992: on my return from work that day I found that the post had brought a most cryptic letter. Could I confirm my maiden name and my address in 1977?

It was from The Children's Society Adoption Project and was asking me to get in touch with them. I knew instantly that it had something to do with my little girl who I had given up for adoption 15 years before.

I telephoned the agency and was told that my daughter wanted to get in touch and that the counsellor, Pat, would call me the next day with the full details. On putting the phone down I burst into tears, even though I was pleased.

It was just so emotional and brought back the whole period of August/September 1976 when I had so wanted to keep my daughter and couldn't.

I was 18 years old at the time. I remembered the pregnancy, leaving home 6,000 miles away in the hope that I would be able to keep her in this country, my parents' support, the birth, caring for her the week that we were together in hospital, feeling like a Judas when I left her at the hospital for the social worker to take her to her foster mother, visiting her at the foster mother's home, trying to find accommodation for a single mother and a child. In the end I believed that adoption was best for my child and hoped that she would understand when she grew older and would want to meet with me. I thought of her often through the intervening years – when she would have started school, on her birthday, at Christmas.

Pat called the next day and asked if I was willing to meet with Yvette (as her adoptive parents had christened her). I did not need to think about it – the answer was a resounding yes. Pat told me that under 18 years of age Yvette could get in touch with me with her parents' consent if I was agreeable.

Pat and I met two days after that initial phone call. In the meantime, I had written a letter to Yvette and when Pat and I met, she gave me a letter from Yvette's mum, photos of Yvette (although none recent – the most recent one reminded me of the elder of my two sisters) and a letter and poem from Yvette which brought tears to my eyes. I felt for Yvette's mum and was so thankful for her support and blessing. I know I would not have felt comfortable if Yvette had not had her parents' support. Naturally they were worried that their daughter could be hurt and I suppose in the beginning saw me as a threat to their relationship with her. As I now had two other children, I could understand their dilemma but I hoped that when they met me they would know that I wasn't a threat to the relationship they had with Yvette. Yvette had been warned that I might not want to meet with her, that when we did meet things might not be as she had wished for or thought. Pat discussed much the same sort of thing with me that afternoon and I was quite aware of the pros and cons. The one thing that worried me was my other children – how would they react?

We had arranged to meet in The Children's Society's office. A friend had agreed to drive me over and as the time grew nearer for her to come and collect me I became more and more nervous. I had stopped biting my nails except for the thumbs and there was nothing left of them to chew on. I would have to buy some more cigarettes on the way as well! This was it – the real thing. Today I was going to meet my daughter for the first time since she was six weeks old. I would find out what (or who?) she looked like – what she was like. I had always hoped that this moment would arrive but was worried that there would be resentment, anger, dislike on Yvette's part. What if I didn't like my baby who had grown up as someone else's girl? It was a discomforting thought.

We got there too early, but Pat told me that Yvette and her mum had got there even earlier. We were in the same building together. I wondered what we would say to each other, how we would react to each other. There was a knock on the door and Pat came in with Yvette – she was so tiny and looked as nervous as I felt. I just hugged her and was so pleased that she hugged me back without any hesitation. We stood looking at each other for a moment or two and then Pat said that she would come back in about 15 minutes to see how things were and bring up Yvette's mum. Yvette had forgotten all the questions she had wanted to ask and I just went through the photographs and other things I had brought with me and we talked about the time we had had together. The photos seemed to break the ice and prevented the nervous silence for the most part although we had moments when we just looked at each other and smiled. I felt at times that I talked 19 to the dozen about absolutely nothing.

In a way I was more nervous about meeting Monica than I was Yvette. I needn't have worried. I find it hard to put into words how I feel about the way she dealt with the whole situation. I am just so thankful that she had the courage, love and trust in her relationship with Yvette to help her go through with it all. She told me that doing the search together had brought her and Yvette closer which made me so glad. Yvette then went to join a family friend who had brought them along to the meeting and left her mum and me on our own for a while. I found her concern for me and my family very touching, when she had had the worry of her daughter meeting with me as well, not knowing how it was all going to turn out.

All too soon it was time for us to say goodbye. We all hugged and kissed each other and Yvette's mum and friend walked off to the car while Yvette and I said a final goodbye. I was managing to hold back the tears until I saw the tears in Yvette's eyes as we hugged each other. I wanted to put 15 years of cuddles into that few minutes and didn't want to let her go.

I spent the weekend on a high and couldn't believe that it had actually happened. My Mum called from Zambia that night, along with my sister who Yvette reminded me of. She told me off as she had worried about me all day and then phoned to find me as high as a kite! My brother and youngest sister telephoned me the following morning. The whole family was thrilled that we had met and that all had gone well and were looking forward to when they could meet her. My only regret was that my Dad had died four years previously and would not get the chance to meet her. My Mum said that if my Dad had still been alive he would have put her on a plane so that she could have been with me for that first meeting.

Since that first meeting I have met Yvette's dad and Yvette and I have met on our own. I have now told my children (14 and 11 years old) about their half-sister. Their reactions were pretty much as I had predicted, although Richard was not angry as I thought he would be. Their initial reaction was that it was all a hoax and then Richard went off on his own for a while and didn't talk to me. I was worried that he was angry with me but his main worry was that I would love him less or that I loved Yvette more. Linda had no such worries and was full of questions, wanting to read the letters and see the pictures. She was not amused when my sister and her family came over for a visit from South Africa and got to meet Yvette before she did! Her words were: "It's not fair, she's my sister and they get to meet her first!". Richard was more anxious than Linda about Yvette's existence and meeting her but they now regard her as a sister and I sometimes feel superfluous.

When Richard and Yvette first met he was quiet but once the ice was broken I was ousted from the room!

I am so grateful to all involved who have made this happen, especially Yvette's parents and Pat – and Yvette for wanting to meet me in the first place. I am grateful also to my family for always being there so that I have been able to share this happy time with them as well."

DIARY OF A REUNION

In this chapter, Lucy describes, in diary form, the process of tracing her birth family. Her account illustrates the day-to-day ups and downs experienced by many people in the same situation.

"THE UNKNOWN"
from July 14th 1989

It is July 14th 1989, and it's a special day for me ... Why? It's my 18th birthday that is being celebrated. I walked straight into a surprise party; I saw people whom I hadn't seen for ages, what a great feeling – it was exhilarating.

The drink was flowing and the food was abundant, then ... out came my birthday cake. It was gorgeous, it seemed such a sin to eat it. Someone handed me a knife and I cut the cake. It wasn't until that moment that I thought about it: I was 18 years old, what does my birth mother think? Is she happy for me or is she sad that she can't be a part of the celebrations? Does she realize or is she oblivious to the fact that July 14th has opened a door that has been closed to me for the past 18 years? ... I can now find my birth mother.

I feel an incomplete person, a part of me is missing ... I don't know who my birth mother is. Who do I look like? ... my mother or my father? Do we share the same likes and dislikes? Do I have any brothers and sisters that I don't know about? There are so many unanswered questions.

For a long time now, I have wanted to trace my birth mother. I haven't really had to think about it, I've just known that it's something I have to do; and on July 14th I started the ball rolling – I wrote to the General Office in Titchfield.

Katie, my counsellor, couldn't have been kinder. She explained why I was being counselled and the effects my finding my birth mother might have on everyone. I told her everything I know about my family background ... she was amazed, saying that the agency that dealt with my adoption obviously believed in the child knowing its origins, as adoption was a fairly taboo subject 18 years ago. So I suppose I have that agency to be grateful for too.

Many adopted people just want to know their original name, but I already knew I wanted to actually meet my mother. I hoped that everything would turn out fine, we would both be friends and she could meet my mum and dad. My birth mother can never be my 'mum', she hasn't loved and hated me, she hasn't brought me up and, most of all, she hasn't known me.

I have put together a picture of my birth mother, it's in the back of my mind; the thing that scares me most is that she won't live up to those expectations. I think of her as being the same as my mum but ... she can't be and won't be. I only hope that she will want to see the daughter she had 18 years ago. It would answer so many questions I have, the foremost being 'why' and 'how'.

After having applied for my original birth certificate, days of agonizing waiting followed. I have another meeting with Katie soon, in which she will be able to tell me some more information she hopes to find. Each day passes ... no certificate arrives, two to three weeks I was told ... it's now the fourth week ... did I send it to the right place? Is there some kind of problem? I really must acquire some patience from somewhere!

Monday 4th December

I am on my way to see Katie. She greets me and we go into the little room, as before. The very first thing Katie says is that she had been able to find a lot of information and there is a fair bit to tell me. That stirs up even more curiosity within me and I'm eager to begin.

Katie starts by saying she's got bits on me, my birth mother, birth father and the background of my adoption. I express dismay at not having received my birth certificate yet. She tells me not to worry as all the information that is on my certificate she is going to tell me anyway. The only thing I don't know is my mother's address at the time of my birth; obviously, we can't begin to trace her without this.

Katie tells me my original name, place of birth etc. (all of which I already knew). Then she goes on to my mother, and I see the address at which she lived. That meant a lot to me. It's hard to explain, but I have always thought of my mother as a person and a name that I know – I wasn't really sure if she was real; sometimes I think it's all just a fantasy.

Katie then went on to my father; he lives in Colchester. It

was a great shock: as my mother lived in Chelmsford, I automatically thought my father would too. I had always believed my father's surname was different to what it actually is. It is a very rare surname. Katie explained the significance of this. It would be easier to trace my father than my mother as her name is more common. Katie asked me what I wanted to do about it. When I first came to her, I was intent on finding my mother, but as my father would be so much easier, I decided to see how far we could get to finding him.

In the telephone directory, there were three surnames the same as my father's listed in Colchester, one of them with my father's initials. Katie thought it would almost certainly be him. She asked me if I wanted her to write a letter to him, or what I wanted to do. By this time, I couldn't believe that things were moving so unbelievably fast. I thought it would all take ages, but knowing he could be at that address in Colchester made me shiver. I knew then that no matter what, I had to find him.

From that meeting, I also learnt that my birth mother had seen a doctor to ask for a termination of pregnancy. I have always been told everything there is to know, but I didn't know this as my adoptive parents were not told, therefore could not pass it on. So when Katie told me, my heart seemed to go bump – it was hard to digest; I might not have had my life. I wondered if my mother is glad the doctor wouldn't terminate her pregnancy. Yet another question. It took me a while to have a good think about all of that.

Katie also told me that after the very first Christmas I was adopted, my mother wrote to the Social Services asking for a photo of me ... that little, seemingly insignificant bit of information really tugged at my heart-strings and the tears started rolling. It must have been just so hard for my mother and father emotionally. I know that they did what they did out of their love for me and I love them for thinking about me like that. It must have been the hardest thing in the world to do and I admire them for the courage and thought they had.

So ... after being told all of this information, I decided that I would like Katie to write to my birth father, saying that we would like to trace him for reasons of the past. She said that if it was him at that address, the response would be immediate.

I was living on tenterhooks from then onwards. I phoned my mum from work every day, asking if she had heard anything. On the following day, my birth certificate arrived. Katie had already told me what it would say, so there was nothing new.

Thursday 7th December

When I came home from work, Katie had phoned. My birth father had phoned her as soon as he received her letter. We had found him. Katie didn't say much on the phone and my mum took the message. Katie suggested that I go to see her the next day, as she could tell me a lot more.

After knowing that Katie had spoken to my father, it aroused a feeling that I can't really explain. Just knowing that she had actually spoken to him, knowing that he existed and wasn't just a figment of my imagination – he was real, not just a name anymore. Then, I wondered what Katie was going to tell me the next day. For the first time since July 14th, I was forced to think of the fact that my father might not want to see me. God, how it hurts to think like that, but it's something I had to face up to; yet somehow I couldn't. My hopes were already on a high, I'd been told not to get my hopes up, but for me ... that's not easy.

That night I hardly slept, the tension and anxiety of not knowing what the next day would bring for me.

I decided that I would like it if my mum would come with me and just be there if I needed her. The walk from the car park to the Social Services was the worst walk ever, my nervousness seemed to increase with every step. By the time we reached Katie's office, I thought I would explode – I was so nervous.

Katie started by saying that my father had telephoned her as soon as he had received her letter yesterday. He wanted to see me. At last, the nervousness erupted in the tears that followed. I had waited 18 years to hear those words. He had asked a lot of questions, to which Katie would give no answers: what do I look like? Am I small?

Katie said that my father was quite emotional as he started to talk. My mother and father did get married but ended up getting divorced. That upset me a bit, but knowing that they were married was enough – at least they meant something to each other. My father had got re-married and has two children by this marriage. He is now going through a divorce.

Katie went on to say that she had a letter from him to me. She left me alone to read it. Of course, I had a good sob – for my father and the rough deal life had dealt him; for the sheer fact that he is my father; and, most of all, for the past 18 years.

I found out that my birth mother lives in Holland. I don't know what I expected to happen when Katie told me this. I had no feelings whatsoever, and that worried me. I was more worried about when I could meet my father.

I went home that night and read my father's letter time after time after time, I didn't let go of it all evening. Knowing that he had written it, he had put the words together from what he feels. The feeling at having that letter is yet another emotion I don't know how to explain. Let me try though ... it's simply something from my father to me that's between us. Those are the only words I can think of. I shall keep it forever.

Friday 8th December
I went to work, my mind wasn't on it though; the curiosity of having my father's phone number was too much for me. The need to call him, and acting on what my heart said ... I phoned him.

I won't write each and every word we said to each other, it was an emotional time for us both. I'm glad I phoned him though, I needed to hear for myself his voice and to satisfy the need to know that he is real.

Saturday 9th December
Since that phone call yesterday, I have re-lived every word of it, not a minute of the day goes by when I am not thinking of my father. The need to meet him now is just so intense, I can now put a voice to the name, and I cannot wait until I can put a whole person to the name as well. The only consolation to the way I am feeling at the moment is that my father is going through the same thing. It helps to know that we are in this together. I can look forward to our meeting.

Wednesday 13th December
I shall meet my birth father this afternoon. I didn't get any sleep last night, I kept trying to think how it would be and what I would say to him.

I don't know how I felt today; sometimes I was like a child who had just been let loose in a sweet shop, sometimes I felt today is some kind of turning point in my life – someone I haven't known or had for 18 years ... I now have. Other times, I was simply nervous and had 'butterflies' galore, as they say.

I was to arrive half an hour before my father, as I wanted to have a quick word with Katie. As I was walking up the stairs, I suddenly thought to myself, the next time I walk down these stairs, I shall know who my father is. Is this really what you want, I asked myself, but I knew the answer to that and have done for these past 18 years.

I was in Katie's office when the call came to say my father had arrived. She went to introduce herself to him and left him waiting in a room while she came to collect me. By this time, I was so nervous I was getting all my words muddled up and stupid things like that. Katie said, "if it's any consolation, he's nervous too". It wasn't! The walk from room to room seemed to take ages, then Katie opened the door to my father. He was looking out of the window. Katie said something and he turned round. The next thing I knew we were in each other's arms. This was the moment I had waited 18 years for. Wow ... just what a powerful feeling it was. I don't know how long we stood there like that. The tears were flowing, neither of us could talk.

Eventually, we let go and sat down. The following hour and a half flew by; it was all thoughts, feelings, emotions and questions of the past 18 years. My father told me all about his life – my mother and him, my adoption. He seemed to just open up and tell everything.

This man who was sitting next to me, holding my hand, was my father. I could hardly believe it was true. I shall always remember that first moment we saw each other. As soon as he turned round, I knew I loved him.

Saturday 16th December

I am meeting my father again today. The nerves are persisting once again, I guess they will for some time yet.

We wandered through the park ... just walking. Then we went to have a cup of coffee. My father showed me a picture of my birth mother. When I say that I have a picture of my mother in the back of my mind, I don't mean a picture of her face, but a picture of what she'll be like in character and personality. But just seeing a picture of her ... she's so beautiful. A lot of emotions seemed to well up inside me during that moment. This woman, whom I don't know, carried me for nine months – she gave birth to me. Knowing I was a part of her hardly seems possible. None of this seems possible – I keep thinking that it's all a dream, in a minute I'll wake up and my father won't be there anymore.

Wednesday 20th December

I woke up this morning and I think something just flipped. I didn't know just how much more of all this I could take. I can't really explain what it was all about. Every time I met with my father I felt guilty: what must my mum and dad be thinking? I wasn't telling them everything, as I thought it would make them feel worse. All of this not telling wasn't doing anyone any good, so we talked about it – my mum, dad and I. Just getting our feelings out in the open really helped us all.

When I first went to see Katie, she didn't know how long it would take to find my birth parents: it could take months, years, or it could take only days. Obviously, I hoped for the latter, but I didn't believe it. So when my father contacted Katie within a week of beginning ... it was a shock. I didn't believe it then and still don't think it's really true. After 18 years of wanting and waiting, all of a sudden I've no more waiting and I've got what I want.

For 18 years, I have been dreaming of what my first meeting with my birth parents would be like. I had, I thought, prepared myself for everything. I suppose, really, it's a bit like when a loved one dies – no matter how you prepare yourself for it, when it happens it's a shock and you are not really prepared at all. I think it was a bit like that.

The only mum and dad and family I have ever known is the family I have always had. Why should it be any different? All of a sudden, I have my birth father, I discover an unknown family: aunts, uncles, cousins and a brother and sister. I am over-flowing with curiosity and love, I suppose, and I can't wait to meet them all. But is seems weird that I am a part of people who I have never met before.

Thursday 21st December

I went to see Katie the other day and we have spoken to my father, who knows my birth mother's sister. My next step is to meet my mother. Then, and only then, will I be a complete person. My father has given Katie her sister's address, he doesn't know my mother's address. I have written a letter to my mother, saying that I would very much like to meet her. Katie is still waiting to hear from her, but it is Christmas and the post is not the same at this time of the year.

Monday 25th December

Christmas day was a funny day this year. It's a time for families to be together and enjoy themselves. I was with my family and I was enjoying myself, but a little bit of that enjoyment was tinged with a little bit of sadness. I just wished that, by some twist, I could have seen my father for a short while and spent a little time with him, but I knew deep down that wish would not come true.

****

Wednesday 27th December
I went to see where my father lives. I just could not believe where it was. Literally, just around the corner from my Nan's house. The amount of times I have been so close, yet so far away, it is really uncanny. It was nice to see his house and to know that he actually does live there.

Thursday 28th December
Father came to meet my mum and dad. I don't feel that I can really say a lot about that meeting because, although I was involved, in another way I wasn't. It's not my feelings that were important, it's my mum and dad's and my birth father's feelings that count. I felt that the meeting went really well. I didn't really expect anything, but I knew nothing would go wrong.

I have now met with my father several times and each time we discover new things about each other; we're bound to, I suppose ... 18 years is a long time, there is still a lot we don't know about each other – maybe we never will ... I don't know.

Every time we meet, somewhere along the line my mother is always spoken about. I suppose it's on both of our minds, the fact that sooner or later I shall meet her. My father is optimistic that I shall meet her soon, but I am not so sure. She has a family, some of whom don't know about me; she will, no doubt, have to tell them now. Am I making it hard for her?

To tell you the truth, I am so scared of meeting her. I was scared of meeting my father, but it wasn't quite like I am feeling now. I don't really know why it should be any different at all, but it is and I just wish I knew why it feels like this. Maybe meeting her will answer that question, I don't know. The need within me to meet my mother is just so great that I think I would go to any ends for that to happen.

I think that my father is scared that when I meet with my

132

mother, I won't want him anymore. That won't ever happen and I have told him this, but how can I expect him to believe me – he has only known me for two weeks.

Both my birth mother and father have and always will be a part of my life. I have never thought of them in the way that 'they didn't want me, so I don't want them'. I have always known that they did what they did out of their love for me. Though I haven't known them for my whole life, they have always meant something to me.

I don't really think that any of us can fully understand what the other is going through: not me, not my adoptive parents, nor my birth father.

We can try to understand what the other is going through, but do we really?

I read somewhere in a book that when you've found your birth parents, it's a feeling like being in love and wanting to spend every minute with that person. That is exactly how I am feeling at the moment. Our time together is never long enough, I just want to sit and talk with my father until we know everything there is to know about each other.

I know that some people feel that adopted children shouldn't be able to trace their birth parents, but obviously those people have never known what it feels like not to have a single person in the world to whom you are related by blood. Trivial as it may seem, blood, genetics and natural origins arc obviously significant, otherwise adopted children wouldn't feel the need to find out who they are.

****

Tuesday 2nd January 1990

The celebrations for the New Year went, as always, with a lot of laughs, but once again I felt the need to be with my birth father as the clock struck the last ten seconds of 1989.

I spoke to my father, John, on the phone today; he had also felt the same as me last night. We seem to be so close and yet we are still so far away.

People seem to say that the bond that forms between a mother and child is something quite unique, yet they never seem to mention the bond between father and child. Before I had even met my father, I loved him, there has always been something there. And the day we first set eyes on each other was when that bond started growing even stronger.

I meet with Katie tomorrow, she may well have heard from my mother by then. I don't know why, but I seem to be really nervous about tomorrow – I suppose it's because of my lack of patience. I really do hope there is some kind of step forward with my mother.

Wednesday 3rd January 1990

I have just returned from a meeting with Katie – she has spoken to my birth mother's sister, Rachel. Rachel is the person that told my mother about me. The day I met my father for the first time is the day my mother and her family returned to England for good. I find it remarkable to believe. I just seem to have had so much luck so far, how much longer will it go on for?

After my birth mother was greeted with this news, apparently she was very emotional, but she does want to see me, that's the main thing. My father has sent Rachel a picture of me to pass on to my mother. Rachel said I look so much like my mother did when she was my age.

I have sent her a letter, via Rachel, which she should have now received. So it's now just a matter of time until she calls, which hopefully won't be too long. I don't know how much longer I can wait.

Tonight, I went to meet John's sister, Kate. Once again, my nerves were persisting – I was going to meet my aunt and cousins.

Kate was really nice; she has three lovely little children. I saw some more old photos and she told me about my birth mother. They all loved her, said she was a wonderful person. God, how much longer must I wait?

Yesterday, I met my half-sister and -brother, Julia and James. They are lovely children. So weird to think of them as my brother and sister. How can they be? I haven't known them. I haven't argued with them. I haven't fought with them. Am I really their sister?

Saturday 6th January

I telephoned Katie to find out if she had heard from Caroline, my birth mother. She hadn't, so she said she would phone Rachel, Caroline's sister. It appears that Caroline wants to meet me, but she is a bit apprehensive at the moment – she doesn't feel ready for it.

Right now, I can't stop myself from crying. Half of what I am feeling I don't know how to explain to anyone, I don't even seem to be able to write it down. I don't know what's happening to me. It's the not knowing that's tearing me apart. I don't know how much longer I can go on like this. People keep telling me that I must be strong. How can I? I have never felt so weak and miserable in my whole life.

Maybe my wanting to see Caroline is just being selfish; she has what she wants – a husband, a family – and she is happy. Perhaps I am just an unwanted intrusion that she'd rather forget about.

I can't even begin to imagine what she must be going through at the moment. She must be going through hell, but then it's not easy for me either. I just couldn't bear it if she said 'no' to me. She is my mother, I am her daughter ... what more can I say?

At the moment, I feel as if I am just living these days in a trance. I am happy when I am with my father and I love my mum and dad, but the rest of the time it's just routine. If I could just hide away in a corner until Caroline would see me, I think I would. Silly as it sounds, everything else is meaningless at the moment. I don't know what's happening to me, I seem to be going to pieces. She's breaking my heart. Maybe I have done what she was hoping I wouldn't do – I've found her.

I think, deep down, that I was a little bit jealous of Julia and James. They have had my father; he has loved, hated, cared for and looked after Julia and James. Why not me? I know the answer to that question really, but I still have to ask myself.

Tuesday 9th January

Well, it's another day to live through. I just wish I had a date or something to look forward to, but there's nothing. Why won't she see me? Meeting her has become like an obsession to me. Maybe I'll phone John and meet him for an hour at lunch – that would help, I think.

Later

I managed to get through today. I did meet John for lunch after all – he says I must give Caroline time. I think that I have now calmed to the idea that I must wait; Caroline must do the running, not me. I can just look forward to knowing that one day I shall meet her. That is what keeps me going.

Thursday January 11th

John came round to my house last night. It was really nice. I'm so glad that everyone gets on together, I didn't want him to go. I think that I have now resigned myself to the fact that meeting Caroline is going to take time. I think it's because I'm not in control of the situation. When I found John, I was in charge; everything went at my pace, which was fast! But I can't control what's happening with Caroline. I now know that she will see me, but how can I expect to just enter her life and her accept it?

****

Sunday 14th January
I don't think I will ever be a part of my birth mother's life. How can I be? She has her life, I have mine. Perhaps she feels threatened by me, maybe she doesn't want to lose everything now that she has obviously found happiness. I am glad that I have found my birth father and am going to meet my birth mother, as I know that I wouldn't be satisfied until I had, but there are times when I wish that perhaps I hadn't started to dig up the past. There are 'fors' and 'againsts' for everything in life.

I don't know what I want from my father. I don't know how often I should see him – I don't want to rush things and spoil it all. Who do I hurt each time I see my father? I don't want to upset my mum and dad – no way, I love them; but I don't know how much is enough and when to stop. I feel as if my life has now been split into two. Sometimes I wish there was some kind of law telling you how to go about handling things once you have found your birth parents. But no two people in this whole wide world are the same, so that wouldn't work.

Wednesday 17th January
I went to see Katie again. She told me that she had phoned Rachel last Monday. Two days later, my birth mother phoned Katie. That was all I needed – at least I knew now that she existed and that someone I know has spoken to her.

Katie said she sounded kind but also very frightened. She does want to meet me, but she isn't sure that she is ready for it yet. I can understand that. Katie said that my mother said she would write a letter and send a photo. Once again ... every day I wait by the letterbox. I have written her a letter. I just hope I said the right things ... whatever they are.

After seeing Katie, I went to see John. I don't think that I should have gone really. After Katie had told me that she had spoken to Caroline, I thought it made me feel better, but it obviously didn't because I was in one hell of a mood when I stepped into John's house. Everything he said, I jumped on. He said he didn't know what to say, but felt he should say something. I think that I didn't want to tell him too much about Caroline because I don't want to upset him any more. I don't know what to say and what not to say. It must look to him that I am shutting him out; I am not, I just want to do the right things and say the right words. Now that I know I will actually meet Caroline, I can't wait until that day. I dream about what it will be like; I know that it will be soon, but it has to be when she is ready – I can wait. I get nervous just thinking about it.

****

Friday 19th January
I got what I was waiting for ... a letter from Caroline. I just sat and stared at the envelope for a couple of minutes. She has sent me a recent photo of herself. The letter was short but lovely, it was just what I wanted to hear from her ... she wants to see me, but just needs time to sort her feelings out. I can understand that. I can't believe that she has actually written those words, I keep reading it over and over again. I really am so lucky to have found both my mother and father.

But I feel loyalty towards my parents and I don't want to hurt them. My mum and dad are really supportive. They must be going through hell and I realize that, deep down, I must be breaking their hearts, but I don't know what to do.

I phoned Katie today to tell her what Caroline had said in her letter, as she didn't know. With the letter, Caroline sent a short note to Katie, saying that she would get in touch again at the end of February. I really do feel a lot better after having got her letter. I think I just needed to hear first-hand from Caroline that she wanted to see me. I feel as if I am a stone lighter – I was so worried that she didn't want to see me, and now I know she does.

I watched a programme on adoption; one of the adopted children who had found her birth mother said that now she felt a complete person – before she had found her mother, a part of her had been missing. But how can she feel whole until she has found her father?

****

Tuesday 23rd January

I spent the day in London as I had an interview for a job. My father, John, had said that he would phone me tonight. I waited and waited but the phone didn't ring. I think that's where I have got it all wrong – he has his life to lead and I have mine. But why did I feel let down when he didn't ring? Maybe I should stop being so selfish.

Friday 26th January

John came round to my house in the evening for a couple of hours. At the moment, my mind is overflowing with thoughts and feelings that I don't really know how to explain. I still cannot relate to John being my father. My dad is old enough to be John's father, because the dad I have now is and will be the only dad I will ever have. It seems totally unreal that this 37-year-old man whom I have never met before, is my father. He is totally different to my dad – hair, size, etc. I guess I imagined all fathers to be like my dad, that is maybe why I find it hard to accept.

Since meeting John on December 13th, I have found little things about him that I don't like; no doubt he has found the same about me, but I want those little bits to go away because I want to like him. I suppose, if I thought about it, there would be little things about my mum and dad that I don't like, but simply because they are my mum and dad, I don't think about it – I take it for granted I suppose. This is exactly what worries me about Caroline; I think I have built up in my mind what a perfect person she will be. I know really that that is just a fantasy but I can't think any other way. Over the past 18 years, various thoughts and feelings that I have felt have been kept in that hole in my heart and I am afraid that when I meet her, I will just overflow.

Having found my birth father, and knowing that I am going to meet my birth mother, maybe I wish that I had left it for a little longer before trying to trace them both. But yet if someone had suggested that to me on my birthday, I think I would have just laughed and said "I'm ready for this, I can handle it". Not once did I ever think it wouldn't work, it hurt me too much to think like that. I thought that I was ready for all of this upheaval ... but, looking back, I don't think I was. I simply did not realize that it would be as difficult as this, for everyone. As things are turning out, I have a little time to think about where I want Caroline to be in my life. I would like her to be a friend to me ... but only time will tell.

****

Monday 29th January
I think I have just come back down to earth with a tremendous bump, hence my moodiness with everyone. Since December the 13th, I believe I have been on such a high. It couldn't last forever and today I think I bounced back into reality. I believed that finding and meeting my birth father was such a wonderful thing. It is, but it's not all it's cracked up to be. I suppose it's just like meeting a new friend. I have been trying to sort things out in my mind today, trying to look at things realistically. But if I could turn back the clock and do things again, I don't suppose I would change a single thing, as my curiosity would no doubt lead me in the same direction.

****

Wednesday 7th February
I went round to John's house for a couple of hours. I haven't seen him for quite a while. It just didn't seem the same. Even when we talk on the phone, it's changed. I don't know why this should be ... but up until three weeks ago, everything was fine; now, it just seems like a dampener has been put on things. I want it to go away. I want it to be like it was, but I don't think that will happen. When I used to meet John before, we both had plenty to talk about, but now I find that I just don't know what to say – what's happening?

Monday 12th February
On Sunday, yesterday, John brought his children round for tea. I wanted him to meet my boyfriend and I wanted my mum and dad to see the children. It all seemed to go well to me – the children seemed to really make themselves at home and I hope they enjoyed themselves. As for John, I hardly spoke to him during the time he was here, so nothing is solved – he just left saying he would phone me.

My mum and I always seem to be at loggerheads. Just

lately, I have been on the defensive with everyone – my mum and dad, my boyfriend and John. I know what the problem is – well, I think I do; I need to talk so much, there is just so much being kept inside me that I feel as if I'll explode soon. But having said that, I can't talk, the words are all in there but I don't know how to say them.

I hope I shall meet with Caroline soon. I don't know if that will help things or make them worse. I feel that I have done John a favour by finding him. I feel as though I am his friend when really I think it should be the other way around. Maybe that's where the problem lies? When I found John, I literally blocked everyone else out of my life - my mum and dad, boyfriend Justin. But now, it seems that I have let everyone back into my life and now I'm blocking John out. I can't seem to find a happy medium anywhere.

****

Monday 19th February

I had arranged to meet John tomorrow evening and take him to meet my Nan. Tonight he phoned and asked me if I minded if we didn't go. There was no explanation – "there's a letter in the post". I was so looking forward to taking him to meet my Nan ... obviously he wasn't. I'm really beginning to wonder what I am doing wrong with him. I just wish things would go back to how they were a month ago. I don't know which way to turn now. I want to be happy. I should be – I'm 18 years old. I should be having the time of my life.

Tuesday 20th February

I still haven't had the promised letter. On the train journey to work today, I was trying my hardest to try and work things out in my mind. When I began all of this, when I opened these doors that had been closed for 18 years – before I even opened the first door – I knew that I wouldn't be happy until I had gone straight through and opened the very last door: Caroline. The word 'father' hadn't even sprung into my mind. Then ... all of a sudden I was led off-track, and a door I had expected to stay closed was staring open at me. Perhaps that is one of the reasons why I am like I am at the moment. Two months ago, I was on cloud nine – Caroline had been forgotten for a while. Then, things slowed down and Caroline shifted back into my thoughts again.

I briefly phoned John today – I don't know why, but I make impulsive decisions and act on them immediately! As usual, we didn't have much to say to each other; he just said that he didn't want to see me until he had sorted out his own feelings about everything (his divorce, etc.) He said that I have made a good life for myself and that I don't need him spoiling it with his problems – now what the hell is that supposed to mean? At the moment, I get the feeling that John and I are just going to fizzle out and these past two months will just be 'another couple of weeks in a lifetime'. That is not what I want to happen, but I really can't tell what John wants. I just don't know what direction we are going in. I keep thinking of the first times we were getting to know each other – why won't those times come back, please?

****

Wednesday 28th February
Katie phoned. Caroline had phoned her yesterday morning and she wants to meet me on Monday. I didn't know what to say when Katie told me that. I was well and truly gobsmacked! I don't think it has sunk in that I am going to meet her on Monday. I have spoken to John and he knows that Caroline has contacted Katie but I haven't told him that I am meeting her on Monday. I don't know if that's doing the right thing or not.

****

Monday 5th March
Well, today is D-Day and surprisingly enough, although I am nervous, it's not like it was before I met John; perhaps, at long last, I have found some patience. I am looking forward to meeting Caroline. It will soon be all over – all that build-up and in one hour it will be over.

****

It was lovely meeting with Caroline, we were both quite tearful. At least I am not the only soppy one around! We hugged each other; the very first thing she said to me was "you look like John". Our meeting lasted just over an hour. It was totally different to the meeting I had with John. I heard

John's life-story in five minutes; Caroline and I just seemed to talk about things in general. I learnt a bit about her family and I talked about mine. I saw a photo of her two little boys. They look lovely. We have exchanged addresses and will meet again soon.

As for John, he said he would phone yesterday, but still nothing. In a way I am glad, because I didn't want to have to lie to him about today. John has hurt me. I don't see why he should shut me out because he has got problems. He and I happened too fast, it was 'give all at once' and now everything has gone flat. I want to resurrect that.

Tuesday 6th March

I have, amongst copying, filing and typing, been trying to figure out my meeting with Caroline yesterday. The only thing Caroline really said that related to what happened 18 years ago was that she is glad she did what she did as she can see now that I have had a happy life. She asked me if I thought she had done the right thing. I really didn't know what on earth to say, I just sat there and tried to say something. How can I answer that question?

Other than that, Caroline didn't say anything about my adoption etc., and I was longing to put to her all the questions I have, but I just didn't seem able to ask. Perhaps Caroline finds it too difficult to talk about it all, or maybe it's because she wants to forget about John. It just all seemed to be small-talk yesterday.

I came out of my meeting with Caroline yesterday feeling different to when I came out of my meeting with John. I don't know why I felt different and I am not really sure what that different feeling was.

I would hope that one day, Caroline and I will be able to look back on all of this and see how we got to know each other; what I want from Caroline is a friend – nothing more, nothing less, simply a friend. From John I would like the same thing, but I don't know what John wants.

I think I thought that once I had met Caroline, I would be a complete person – which, in a sense, I am I suppose. I thought that all the little bits of unhappiness everyone gets in their life would go out of the window and I would be on cloud nine for the rest of my life ... how stupid, but I couldn't see beyond that. I can no longer dream about what Caroline is like, and I think I will miss that. I truly believed that meeting with her would be wonderful - a change in my life – but, as I have heard many times before, it's not all it's cracked up to be. I think that now I just want to calm down, think about things and try to move a bit slower – get to know Caroline and be friends with her. Katie is still going to keep in contact with me. She has been so good.

Thursday 8th March

I met John today. Everything seemed to be going fine. We went for a coffee and it wasn't until we were heading back towards the car that he asked me how my meeting with Caroline had gone. So I told him all that I wanted to tell him and then, quite unexpectedly, he said that he knows Caroline's address. When he said that, it was like I had been physically hit down. All I could see was whatever I might have had with Caroline, tumbling down around me. This was the final straw, the moment I had hoped would never come. Obviously, he'll contact her; she will think I have given him her address and that will be that: the end of the beginning.

After John had brought me home, I just felt like crying; but I didn't – it doesn't help anyone.

Friday 9th March

I phoned Katie to ask for her advice on what to do. Immediately, she suggested that I write to Caroline, telling her that John had her address and the reasoning etc. She felt that Caroline had a right to know, especially so that if John did contact her, she wouldn't think it was me that gave him her address.

I sent the letter and I heard nothing. I could only assume the worst and I was so worried.

Friday 16th March

A letter came from Caroline, telling me not to worry about John having her address and saying that she and her husband would like to meet me the weekend I had suggested. That was a relief!

****

Friday 23rd March

I am going on holiday for a week. Maybe things will be better when I come home. Perhaps a break will make everything alright.

Wednesday 18th April

It's been a long time since I wrote anything in here. I have still had feelings, but I suppose they have not been negative, troubled feelings – which is perhaps why I haven't felt the need to write it all down.

Last Saturday, I met Caroline and her husband. She showed me some photos of her family. It was nice to see her again (for the second time) but I can honestly say that it wouldn't bother me if I never saw either my birth mother or father again. I would never have said that a few weeks ago, but I feel that somehow something within me has changed. I would never have been a complete person until I had found both of them, but I have been lucky and now I feel that I have done what I set out to do. I know who they are, what they are, what they look like and I have learnt a little bit of the reasoning behind my adoption. I have my life to lead; I have goals in my life and I hope that I will reach them.

I haven't heard from John for a month now, and Caroline for a week, and I am not at all bothered. I have, at last, got my priorities right. There is just one more thing that I ask for and that is for my mum and dad to meet Caroline; then and only then will I honestly be able to say that I have totally quenched my thirst. So, until then, I will keep this diary open.

****

Sunday 13th May

Last week I wrote a letter to Caroline, asking her if maybe sometime she would like to meet my mum and dad. I sent the letter and didn't think any more of it. I didn't suggest that we meet up again, simply because it doesn't worry me anymore.

Anyhow, a couple of days later, there was a phonecall for me at work – it was Caroline's husband. I didn't know who it was when he first said his name. He told me that Caroline had got my letter and she was worried because she doesn't want to meet my parents yet. He gave me their home phone number and suggested maybe I could phone her. I was really angry at the fact that he had phoned me at work – that's interfering with my life and I don't want that. I knew as soon as he gave me the number that I wouldn't phone Caroline. I couldn't – don't ask me why.

Had I had her phone number a few months ago, I would have been straight on the phone, but not now. So I wrote her a letter instead. The only reason I suggested a meeting with my mum and dad was because I know that they would very much like to meet her, and so that I could then forget the whole thing and look forward. Now I feel that I have to carry on with this until she meets my mum and dad.

John phoned me one night last week when I was out. Apparently, he was talking with my mum, saying that he thought I sounded distant last time I spoke to him. That made me so angry. How the hell does he have the nerve to talk to my mum about me like that; he doesn't even know me.

I just can't be bothered with all of this anymore; I can honestly say that I have well and truly quenched my curiosity and now I just wish it could all be in the past. I am longing to ask Caroline so many questions about my adoption etc., but she hasn't spoken about it at all on the only two occasions I have seen her. Stupid little questions that may seem silly to you but yet are important to me, like what was it like when I was born. I can't ask my mum that as she can't answer it. But hopefully one day I will have kids and I would like to know what she went through when she had me. Was she happy, sad? Maybe I will never know the answers, I don't know anymore.

****

Tuesday 22nd May

At the weekend, I got a letter from Caroline, saying that she would like to meet my parents and that maybe when the weather improves, we could meet at a pub with a garden, and she and her husband could bring their children. I have replied, saying that that would be nice.

Last night, I went to visit a couple of friends of mine whom I haven't seen for over a year. They were eager to know all about my adoption, so I told them the whole story and what I feel towards my birth parents now. I have said that it wouldn't worry me if I never saw them again. But, as Bridget pointed out to me, you can't just open the door into someone's life and promptly shut it in their face and say that you've had all you want, and goodbye. What a selfish person I must be to want to do that. I'm beginning to wonder what is really going on inside me.

****

Tuesday 18th December

It is the first time for ages that I have actually sat down and thought that perhaps I ought to round this off a bit. Whatever I write now will probably be a bit out of perspective as I am not writing my feelings down as I experience them. I am just trying to remember how I felt way back then. It seems ages ago, but a few months back in June, my mum and dad and brother met Caroline, her husband and children. We all met in a pub garden – a reasonably neutral place. Finally, my mum and dad were meeting my birth mother, which I had wanted to happen for such a long time. Everything seemed to go really well, there were no difficult silences in the conversation or anything. I was also pleased that my birth mother, Caroline, could see us together as a family and she could see just how much they all mean to me, and that I didn't just find her because I wasn't happy at home.

A lot of things have happened since then. I have now started my three-year nurse training and am having the time of my life. I love coming home to my family every now and again.

I can honestly say that since I have moved away, I have not thought about Caroline or John at all. I have written once to John, just to let him know my new address, but I have heard nothing whatsoever. I have had one letter from Caroline and I have sent them both Christmas cards.

Caroline has invited us over to her house for a Christmas drink. Perhaps we'll go, I don't know yet. Since I have been away, Caroline has visited my mum here at home. My mum said that it was a really nice visit and they chatted away to each other without the slightest hesitation. I am glad my mum is happy with all of this as well.

I don't know what else to say, except that I have, in one way and another, enjoyed writing this. I look back on it and it's really hard to believe that I ever went through all of this and came out relatively unscathed. It is certainly an experience I will never forget, but will look back on it as another chapter in my life.

I hope that reading through the many emotions that I experienced may help someone some day.

Lucy's adoptive mother presents her perspective on her daughter's story.

Love of a Special Kind

It was her 18th birthday, she hadn't particularly wanted a party but how could we let this occasion pass without somehow marking it. She is, after all, the only daughter we will ever have. After some deliberation, a surprise barbecue was our idea, with close family and friends. It worked, she hadn't a clue and just how it was kept such a secret we shall never know. Her face as she came into the garden that night was something I'll never forget. Her friends had all managed to avoid the truth about what they were doing that evening. It was great! But as with such moments, past years came flashing back with a certain clarity, as did that summer day in 1971 when a tiny bundle was placed into my arms. That bundle, over the coming years, was to evoke such feelings and emotions as I never knew existed. It was, of course, pure joy that afternoon, mixed with many uncertainties and small fears – so similar, to some extent, to those on her 18th.

We had just over 24 hours' notice that we were to have a beautiful little daughter, and on that day I wept buckets for the young people who had produced this child and were unable, through sheer circumstances, to keep her as their own. I also panicked, realizing the freedom my husband and I had had was to disappear – was this honestly what I wanted? It really wasn't too late to say no.

Of course the next day dawned and any doubts had been completely obliterated by an excitement and longing. The moment had arrived and I have no words to explain how I felt just then. Suffice to say, as many feel on a cloud the day they marry, so too did we the day we got her.

Love was instant, no searching, no wondering, it just happened.

From that day, we had always promised to be totally honest and tell her all about her 'beginnings'. We also faced the fact that in later life she would probably wish to find out more, and that we would give her our support.

As with many preparations, how prepared are we? I thought I had spelt it out to myself; after all, I had had 18 years to do this. But, as with the death of a loved one, it still came as a tremendous shock.

Right now I am experiencing emotions I didn't know I had, or that my daughter would have – oh boy!, they are just so powerful.

Our moment of truth begins this week when she will meet with her birth father, and from this moment on I will try to record how I feel in order that maybe some day this may help others to understand themselves a little more clearly.

Fortunately, there have always been mountains of love in this house and we're all fairly capable of showing it. Here's hoping it will see us through this time.

8th March 1990

From that day to this, I have not put pen to paper, and much has happened. But I will now try to take a lead and some inspiration from my daughter's own diary of events.

There have been many 'ups and downs' in this house since, and some moments which have been almost too difficult to cope with.

Lucy met her birth father, which was to prove a very emotional experience for both of them, and afterwards for us as a family. As Lucy's parents, we had many doubts and fears, especially about her meeting a man we knew nothing about. We knew too that we had to let her go, and to be so very guarded with our warnings and advice. Under no circumstances must we make her feel guilty, or imply this was something she shouldn't be doing.

So the father and daughter relationship began. It was so intense in the first few weeks. In a way ironic, because it had only ever been her mother she was anxious to trace, but circumstances revealed him first and there were, for a time, no more thoughts on her mother. The intensity of this new relationship was consequently to provoke uncertainties, insecurities, guilt feelings and ultimately many rows and tears, but I have to say much love too. A true test of just how much relationships can withstand.

There were moments of a special closeness and others of a great distance between all of us; times when we managed to talk about what was happening in our lives and some when we obviously found it too much of an interference with each other's privacy.

Lucy, at this time, was completely obsessed with meeting and being with her birth father. It was so difficult, because you wondered if you would ever become a part of her again.

There were other times when her guilt was inconsolable, possibly because basically she knew she was not in control of all that was happening to her, and that the rows and difficulties were all centred around her.

Lucy's moods have taken enormous swings, often difficult to cope with; at the same time, the rest of the family has been almost 'lost in the crowd': who do we turn to for help?

Often, I would dearly like to have gone away somewhere by myself and tried to sort out what was happening to this once 'laughing happy family', but I always knew that if I was weak, so too was everybody else.

I believe Lucy has not found any of this any easier than the rest of us. I also feel she has, at times, felt that not everything comes up to expectations, but then what dream ever comes 100% true?

I wish that I could add to this epistle my exact emotions throughout, but I'm not sure that I can. For a start, there have probably been too many, and for another I don't think I have understood all of them. However, here are just one or two: fear, possibly, first – fear of losing her; fear for my 'family', which I probably treasure above all; fear, too, for my sanity to prevail; and fear in case events do not turn in the right direction. Another emotion felt is one I didn't know I possessed: jealousy – and for the first time ever I experienced this powerfully; it was that I might have to share this child whom I had so lovingly cared for and nurtured and seen through 18 years of all kinds of moments and to see her perhaps share some experiences that I felt should be ours. How selfish. I had, after all, had her very best years, but there it is – this is how I felt. Another of my emotions was perhaps typical of any mother, and that was over-protectiveness. But how can you help it when you care so very much?

Above all, and throughout these traumas, we know there is as much love for each other as there ever was, but I do pray to God for a stability to return to us; I'm sure at some stage it will.

Very quickly, Lucy was asking us to meet with her birth father. Of course we were willing and probably curious too. So a date was arranged. The meeting went well and was reasonably relaxed, although, strangely, it felt slightly unreal. We learnt many things that night, even a little of what it felt like from his point of view when Lucy was given up for adoption. Above all, we now knew who she was meeting. We were to meet on several occasions.

Her meetings averaged four, five or even six times a week. Sadly, as her parents, we could see a relationship which was to fade almost as quickly as it had begun, but we knew we must remain in the background. As the novelty waned, so the anxiety within Lucy grew as to when and where and if she would be meeting her birth mother. She permanently watched the post and it seemed, at the time, like daily disappointment. Eventually, the letter arrived.

End of March

This was to prove completely different. From the outset, it has been a far steadier, calmer approach. Her birth mother had not found it quite so easy to come to terms with facing a child she knew she had borne and yet did not know. I'm glad she took her time. It will help to show Lucy that time and patience make such a difference, especially with something as deep as this.

Sometimes, when trying to explain to Lucy, I feel so helpless and not always at ease with what I have to say to her, purely, I think, because there are some things I know Lucy must work out for herself. At 18 she is still so tender, but she has to go it alone.

Lucy met with her mother on only one or two occasions, along with her mother's husband, a most supportive fellow. These meetings were pleasant but undramatic. Lucy learnt little of what she really had a great desire to know. Eventually, her mother's family and our own all met for a pub-lunch. This, too, went very well and there was some talk of the difficulties that Lucy's birth mother experienced through her pregnancy and afterwards up until she met and married her now husband. When it was time for goodbyes, both she and I found it very easy just to put our arms around each other; there was no need for words.

Emotions and family atmospheres were just so much easier to cope with.

I haven't said much about T.J. (Lucy's brother), but I do know that he too has not been left unaffected – how could he be? He could, at times, just shut himself away in his room, leave the troubles behind his closed door. I do know he thinks Lucy has made a mistake in 'opening doors', but there, I think, is the logic of a boy who knows he may in later years be opening similar ones.

It is now some time since my thoughts have turned to writing more about the experience that caused so many emotions to us as a family.

First, I have to say that throughout the tears and rows, we have SURVIVED and family relationships have now returned to their former easy, happy state; that if there was anything at all to add, it is that the bond is now even stronger. I feel so lucky, so fortunate, so blessed that it should be so, it proves to me just what the Family is all about and that there is nothing in the world as valuable as love.

Lucy is now a complete person. She is able to go forth and adequately cope in a mature and stable way with her own life, career and future, and above all is just so HAPPY.

I find it difficult to believe that in the depths of her searching we all felt so insecure, but now I am so very proud of each member of my family. We are here, we did make it and we are as one.

Looking back over these notes, however, there is one vital point that I have missed, and why I don't know. Almost without fail, the majority of our rows stemmed from Lucy's unjust behaviour towards her dad – he always took the brunt of her pent-up feelings. She would either not really talk to him at all, or otherwise snipe at him and treat him like a bit of dirt. He never, never turned on her, and Lucy said that somewhere within her, she knew that their relationship was so strong it could take all of this. In retrospect, I am quite certain this was absolutely true.

Three weeks ago now, I met with Lucy's birth mother again, just she and I. We had coffee together, we chatted easily and probably learnt a good deal about each other. It somehow completes the story and was a special moment for both of us.

February 1991

It is now a year since we were in the depths of an experience never to be forgotten. Lucy is now happily ensconced in her nursing career and it all seems like a dream.

Since perhaps the beginning of her career, now some months ago, there has been very little contact between Lucy and her birth parents. Sadly, Lucy and her father ran out of steam, added to which their lives have trodden such very different paths, and, after the initial period, they were quite apparently left with little or nothing to say to each other.

I feel that with her mother, however, the relationship never got off the ground, for reasons I'm not sure about. And yet her mother obviously lives a life akin to our own. I know that Lucy still has questions she would like to ask her mother, but I now wonder if she ever will.

Both my husband and I feel very strongly that we hope Lucy will keep contact, if only a sporadic one: perhaps a letter, a card occasionally. After all, she opened the door – she shouldn't shut it in their faces.

Basically, we know Lucy had to do this just to find the missing piece of jigsaw. I really do understand.

If our experiences can possibly help others who will no doubt tread a similar path, then sharing my feelings will have been worthwhile. No two cases will ever be alike, but knowing someone else has experienced similar circumstances must create a certain affinity. There must be a trust.

CONCLUSION

We hope you have enjoyed reading the various accounts of people's experiences, and have found something that meets your own needs.

If you are personally involved in adoption, you may decide, having read this, that you want to go further. You may decide to seek only information, or to find your birth relatives, or to do nothing.

Your own journey will be unique and although you may encounter similar emotions, difficulties and joys to those recorded in this text, no book can cover the whole range of possible circumstances.

Whatever path you choose, we hope that the people who have shared their experiences and emotions in this book will have offered you some sort of preparation.

Although searching and finding can be an exciting, joyous time, it can rarely be without some pain. Yet despite the difficulties and the trauma of reunion, the majority of people do not regret their decision to search.

However tentative your search may be, once you have begun you cannot go back again or put behind you completely the information you gain. Integrating past and present is no easy task, and it may take several months or years before your life settles down.

Most people who embark on a journey for more information or renewed contact need the support of friends, family and counsellors, so make sure you know what services are available to you. Other members of the adoption circle may also need care and support. You will find a list of useful addresses at the end of this book.

Putting this book together has been a stimulating and informative experience. So many people we have come into contact with have been eager to offer their experiences in the hope that it may help others, and we are very grateful to all those who have contributed.

POSTSCRIPT

The accounts in this book have been written by those involved in baby placements. In the 1960s and 70s, however, several different factors came together that changed the face of adoption. The development of the contraceptive pill and more freely available family planning services led to a decline in the numbers of babies being available for childless couples to adopt. It also became more socially acceptable for single mothers to raise their babies themselves.

The plight of older children who were remaining in residential care provided by local authorities, was highlighted in several research studies (eg. Rowe, J. and Lambert, L. *Children Who Wait*. ABAA, 1973). The needs of these children and the smaller number of babies being placed for adoption led to the move to place older children for adoption. Another development was to place children previously thought 'unadoptable' because of health or behavioural difficulties. Specialist agencies and projects were set up to find permanent homes for such children, who were seen as 'hard to place'.

There was also growing concern about the numbers of black children who were seen to be remaining in the care system. Many professional families offered a home to a black child or a child of mixed parentage rather than see them remain living in a children's home (termed 'transracial adoption'). In the 1960s and 70s there was little effort made to find black families for black children. Many adoptive parents have worked hard to keep their child in touch wich their culture and to give them a positive and clear sense of identity. However, the white adoptive families often had no personal or social links with the black community and in the early days they were not given the information and preparation they needed by adoption agencies to help them deal with issues of race and culture.

Many black adopted children grew up isolated in white middle class areas with no black adult role models. As adults they are clearly seen as black individuals with a white family background and culture. Some black adults have been able to live with this dilemma but others have struggled to learn about their black roots, origins and culture and to gain acceptance for themselves within a black community. For them, the seeking out of a black parent is a vital part of the reconstruction of their positive black self-image.

By listening to black social workers and transracially adopted adults, agencies have learned over the years how essential it is for positive information about culture, race and religion to be given. The Children Act 1989 stresses the importance of considering race, culture and religion when placing children in new families. It also emphasizes the need to take into account the wishes and feelings of families of origin and to work in partnership with them when making placements.

Adoption in the 1990s is therefore very different from the situation under the Adoption Act 1926. The majority of those considered for adoption today are young children with special needs, or older children who are unable to live at home because of abuse, neglect or some other form of family breakdown.

These children often have very real relationships with and memories of some members of their birth family. Many have photographs and life-story books that contain information about why they are separated from their birth family, and many grow up in full knowledge of their early background.

Often there is some form of continuing contact between birth family members, adopters and adoptees, whether through actual visits or by exchanging letters and photographs. This contact may take place directly or through the adoption agency. We do not yet know how this more open and inclusive approach will alter the feelings and needs reflected in this book. Some children have been placed for adoption against the wishes of birth parents. Again, we do not know how this may affect the future needs of the parties involved.

In recent years, inter-country adoption has become a growing issue. Babies and very young children from abroad are sometimes brought to Britain for adoption. Whilst this removes them from what may be seen as their immediate plight, and provides the necessary security, safety and well-being to thrive, there is much debate about how they will be able to obtain a full sense of identity and completeness when they are so far removed from their family and culture. Some children have come with little information about their background; for some the birth date is not even known. The writers in this book reflect how overwhelming the need for information may be for all parties in the adoption circle.

Many birth relatives have come to The Children's Society to ask for information about children placed for adoption. In the last few years, The Children's Society has begun to offer an intermediary service to birth relatives. Many need to know if their adopted child is alive and well and some need to let them know of their interest. The Children's Society are now willing to approach the adopted adult, usually via the adoptive parents to let them know of the birth relative's enquiry so that they can make their own decision about how to respond.

At present, local authorities and adoption agencies have a duty to provide a comprehensive service, but many would say that past services have neglected adoptive parents and birth family members after adoption. Many agencies now understand that adoption is a life-long process, with the making of the Adoption Order being a part of this process rather than an end in itself. The three parties will continue to have some sort of impact on each other, even if there is no contact.

Adoption in Britain has in the past been developed and organized in the main by white workers and agencies. The 'solution' of terminating a child's contact with his/her family and placing him/her with a new one is a specific, perhaps cultural, response to situations where children are unable to live at home. Other cultures have very different ways of dealing with this and we can learn and have learned from other approaches.

There may always be children for whom adoption is the best solution, for instance those who come from irredeemably violent or dangerous families or those where parental abuse perpetuated on children is not acknowledged as such or seen to be a wrong and inappropriate way to bring up a child.

At the time of writing this book, changes to Adoption Law are being planned. We would hope that future legislation will make it a duty for adoption agencies to offer advice and support both before and after adoption to all those involved.

The experience of everyone in the adoption circle points toward the need for agencies involved in arranging adoptions to be flexible and avoid making rigid rules about openness, secrecy or contact. Each situation and the people in it should be treated as individuals and their needs catered for. Compromises may need to be made to accommodate everyone. Honesty and open communication are of paramount importance.

Adoption agencies are learning all the time from the people in the adoption circle and try to put this learning into practice for the future benefit of everyone involved in adoption. We hope that this book will add to that learning.

USEFUL ADDRESSES

The Post Adoption and Care: Counselling and Research Project
The Children's Society
11 Queens Road, Peckham, London SE15 2EZ
tel. 071-732 9089

Offers a counselling service for people who have either been adopted through The Children's Society or have been in its care, and for their respective adoptive and birth families.

The Post Adoption Centre
8 Torriano Mews, Torriano Avenue, London NW5 2RZ
tel. 071-284 0555

Offers post-adoption support and counselling services for adoptive families, adopted people and birth parents whose children were adopted.

BAAF (British Agencies for Adoption and Fostering)
11 Southwark Mews, London SE1 1RQ
tel. 071-407 8800

Provides advisory and training services for member agencies. Also offers information and advice to members of the public.

NORCAP
(National Organization for the Counselling of Adoptees & Parents)
3 New High Street, Headington, Oxford OX3 7AJ
tel. 0865 750554

An organization for adopted people, birth and adoptive relatives. NORCAP provide support and advice as well as an intermediary and tracing service for its members. They also hold a register of adoptees and birth relatives interested in making contact.

PPIAS
(Parent to Parent Information on Adoption Services)
Lower Boddington, Daventry, Northamptonshire
tel. 0327 60295

Acts as an information exchange on all aspects of adoption and a support service for all adoptive families. There are local group contacts throughout the UK.

The Office of Population Censuses and Surveys
The General Register Office, Adoptions Section
Smedley Hydro, Trafalgar Road
Birkdale, Southport PR8 2HH

Co-ordinates the work of local registrars of births, marriages and deaths. Application forms for access to birth records are sent in response to written requests. Also manages the Adoption Contact Register.

Natural Parent Support Group
3 Aldergrove, Normanton, West Yorkshire WF6 1LF
tel. 0924 894076

A self-help organisation for birth parents whose child has been placed for adoption.

After Adoption
2nd Floor, Lloyds House, 22 Lloyd Street, Manchester M2 5WA
tel. 061-839 4930

Offers post-adoption support and counselling services for adoptive families, adopted people and birth parents whose children were adopted.

Family Care
21 Castle Street, Edinburgh EH2 3DN
tel. 031-225 6441

Offers support and advice to adopted people, adoptive families and birth families. Holds the adoption contact register for Scotland.

Church of Ireland Adoption Society
12 Talbot Street, Belfast BT1 2QH
tel. 0232 233885

Makes adoption placements and assessments and offers a post-adoption service.

The Children's Society

The Children's Society is a national voluntary organization of the Church of England and the Church in Wales. It exists to work for children and young people, irrespective of their race or religious belief:
* to help them grow in their families and communities
* to help them take charge of their own lives
* to help them change the conditions that stand in their way.

The Children's Society runs 126 projects throughout England and Wales including:
* family centres and neighbourhood groups in local communities where families are under stress, often feeling isolated and powerless to improve their lives
* independent living units for young people leaving care
* working with young people living on the street
* residential and day care for children and young people with disabilities
* helping children and young people with special needs to find new families
* offering independent guardians ad litem for children involved in care proceedings
* promoting the rights of children and young people.

The Children's Society is committed to raising public awareness of issues affecting children and young people and to promoting their welfare and rights in matters of public policy. It produces a wide range of publications, including reports, briefing papers and educational material.

For further information about the work of The Children's Society or to obtain a full publications list, please contact:
The Publications Department
The Children's Society
Edward Rudolf House
Margery Street
London
WC1X 0JL
tel 071-837 4299; fax 071-837 0211